Professional Development Handbook

Book 1

by Roslyn Denny

Jim Williamson

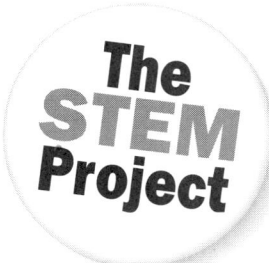

A HOUGHTON MIFFLIN COMPANY
Evanston, Illinois • Boston • Dallas

McDougal Littell: www.mcdougallittell.com
Middle School Mathematics: www.mlmath.com

Acknowledgments

The STEM Project

Middle Grades Math Thematics is based on the field-test version of the STEM Project curriculum. The STEM Project was supported in part by the

 NATIONAL SCIENCE FOUNDATION

under Grant No. ESI-9150114. Opinions expressed in *Middle Grades Math Thematics* are those of the authors and not necessarily those of the National Science Foundation.

Illustrations: page 84, Jeremy Spiegel

Copyright © 1999 by McDougal Littell Inc. All rights reserved.

ISBN: 0-395-89461-1

5 6 7 8 9 10–B–03 02

Table of Contents

How to Use This Handbook . . . . *iv*

Presenting the MIDDLE GRADES Math Thematics Curriculum 1

Philosophy 1

Organization of Material in Student Book 4

Module Themes and Content with NCTM Standards 5

Why Change Mathematics Education? 9

Exploring Math Thematics, Book 1 10

Close-Up of a Section 10

Looking at *Setting the Stages* 29

Looking at Explorations 33

Looking at Technology 47

The Authors' Answers to Reflecting Questions 49

Assessment in Math Thematics 54

Introduction 54

Using the *Math Thematics* Assessment Scales 56

Managing *Extended Explorations* 66

Using Portfolios 72

Math Thematics Assessment Summary 76

Answers to Assessment Questions 78

Implementing the Math Thematics Curriculum 80

Communicating with Parents 80

Cooperative Learning 84

Adjusting for Special Needs 87

Materials List for Book 1 90

Commonly Asked Questions 91

References 93

Scope and Sequence Chart 95

How to Use This Handbook

This handbook serves two purposes. It is intended to be a guide for leaders of *Math Thematics* inservice workshops and a resource manual for teachers using the *Math Thematics* curriculum.

Presenting and Exploring

As an inservice guide, this handbook provides outlines for various workshop formats and the supporting materials required for them. Some of the materials, such as the philosophy overviews and content charts, can be copied from this handbook onto transparencies.

Participants in a workshop should work through the *Math Thematics* explorations and discuss the features of the text. Questions are provided to help facilitate this discussion. We have also included our response to these questions in *The Authors' Answers to Reflecting Questions* (pp. 49–53).

Assessing

An assessment section is also included, which addresses the types of assessment in *Math Thematics,* the management of Extended Explorations (E^2s), and the use of portfolios. This section provides guidance for a workshop leader, as well as a resource for classroom teachers.

Implementing

The last section of this handbook looks at aspects of implementing the *Math Thematics* curriculum, including communicating with parents and adjusting for special needs. Again, this section is applicable as a resource for teachers and workshop leaders.

Workshop Outlines

$1\frac{1}{2}$-Hour Inservice

Content/Agenda	Handbook pages	Other Materials Needed
Philosophy	pp. 1–3	
Organization of Material in Student Book	p. 4	
Close-Up of a Section	pp. 10–28	copies of student pages 218–228, Labsheets 6A, 6B (optional)
Module Themes and Content with NCTM Standards	pp. 5–8	

$\frac{1}{2}$-Day Inservice (approximately 3 hours)

Content/Agenda	Handbook pages	Other Materials Needed
Why Change Mathematics Education?	p. 9	
Philosophy	pp. 1–3	
Organization of Material in Student Book	p. 4	
Close-Up of a Section	pp. 10–28	copies of student pages 218–228, Labsheets 6A, 6B (optional)
Module Themes and Content with NCTM Standards	pp. 5–8	
Purposes of Assessment and Assessment Tools	pp. 54–55, 76–77	
Communicating with Parents	pp. 80–83	

1-Day Inservice (approximately 6 hours)

Content/Agenda	Handbook pages	Other Materials Needed
Why Change Mathematics Education?	p. 9	
Philosophy	pp. 1–3	
Organization of Material in Student Book	p. 4	
Close-Up of a Section	pp. 10–28	copies of student pages 218–228, Labsheet 6A, Lasbsheet 6B (optional)
Looking at *Setting the Stages*	pp. 29–32	paper clips, colored chips, Labsheet 2A
Looking at Explorations	pp. 33–39	marked beans, paper cup, game pieces
Module Themes and Content with NCTM Standards	pp. 5–8	
Assessment		
• Purposes of Assessment and Assessment Tools	pp. 54–55, 76–77	index cards, scissors, rulers, copies of the E^2 labsheet
• Managing *Extended Explorations*	pp. 66–71	*Teacher Assessment Scales*, p. 64
• Using the *Math Thematics* Assessment Scales	pp. 56–65	
Communicating with Parents	pp. 80–83	

2-Day Inservice

Content/Agenda	Handbook pages	Other Materials Needed
DAY 1		
Why Change Mathematics Education?	p. 9	
Philosophy	pp. 1–3	
Organization of Material in Student Book	p. 4	
Close-Up of a Section	pp. 10–28	copies of student pages 218–228, Labsheet 6A, Labsheet 6B (optional)
Looking at *Setting the Stages*	pp. 29–32	paper clips, colored chips, Labsheet 2A
Looking at Explorations	pp. 33–39	marked beans, paper cup, game pieces
Cooperative Learning	pp. 84–86	
Module Themes and Content with NCTM Standards	pp. 5–8	
Looking at Technology	pp. 47–48	
Communicating with Parents	pp. 80–83	
DAY 2		
Assessment		
• Purposes of Assessment and Assessment Tools	pp. 54–55, 76–77	index cards, scissors, rulers, copies of the E^2 labsheet
• Managing *Extended Explorations*	pp. 66–71	*Teacher Assessment Scales*, p. 64
• Using the *Math Thematics* Assessment Scales	pp. 56–65	
Looking at Explorations	pp. 40–46	paper clips, Labsheet 6B
Adjusting for Special Needs	pp. 87–89	
Annotated Teacher's Edition		copy of annotated Teacher's Edition
Materials List for Book 1	p. 90	

Teacher Materials

Teacher's Edition

The *Math Thematics* Teacher's Edition is a complete, full-size student book with annotated answers to all questions and exercises. It also contains Warm-Up Exercises and Closure Questions at point of use along with their answers.

Teacher's Resources

The Teacher's Resources includes four *Teacher's Resource Books* that contain two modules each. Each Resource Book includes:

- Module overview and charts for pacing, planning, objectives, ideas, and materials needed
- Teaching suggestions underneath reduced facsimiles of the student book pages
- Labsheets in blackline master form
- Discussion about the *Extended Explorations* in the student book
- Alternate *Extended Explorations* that can be substituted for each one in the student book
- Warm-Up Exercises and Quick Quizzes for each section
- Practice and Application blackline masters for each section
- Study Guide blackline masters for each section
- Technology Activity blackline master related to each technology page in the student book
- Assessment blackline master—a mid-module quiz and two module tests, Forms A and B
- Standardized Assessment blackline master for each module
- Module Performance Assessment blackline master for each module
- Answers to blackline masters
- English-to-Spanish Glossary (located in the Teacher's Resource Book for Modules 1 and 2)

PRESENTING the MIDDLE GRADES Math Thematics Curriculum

Philosophy

The *Math Thematics* program is a complete middle grades mathematics curriculum designed to implement the National Council of Teachers of Mathematics *Curriculum and Evaluation Standards for School Mathematics*.

Goal of the Program

The goal of the program is to develop math power in all students. To develop math power, we believe students must develop their abilities to:

- Reason logically
- Apply mathematical skills to real-world activities
- Communicate about and through mathematics
- View mathematics as relevant to their lives and connected to other areas
- Understand the connections among the different strands of mathematics and the connections of mathematics to other content areas
- Feel confident in using quantitative and spatial information to make decisions
- Become independent learners with a desire for lifelong learning

Content

To ensure that a complete curriculum is provided, the learner outcomes are organized in traditional strands: *Number, Measurement, Statistics, Algebra, Geometry, Probability, Discrete Mathematics*, and *Problem Solving*. However, the content:

- Is problem solving oriented
- Emphasizes critical thinking and reasoning over rote procedural drill
- Decreases the emphasis on review of "elementary" topics such as whole number computation
- Increases emphasis on data analysis and statistics, proportional reasoning, algebra, geometry, and discrete mathematics

Unifying Concepts

Four unifying concepts, *Proportional Reasoning, Multiple Representations, Patterns and Generalizations*, and *Modeling*, are used throughout the curriculum to help students make connections and build mathematical conceptions.

The ability to reason proportionally, that is, to express one number as a certain multiple of another, provides the basis for understanding the concepts of ratio, rate, percent, proportions, slope, similarity, scale, linear functions, and probability.

Working with different representations of concepts helps students understand mathematical ideas by providing for different styles of learning. Multiple representations connect topics such as coordinate systems and functions, fraction-decimal-percent representations, and geometric representations of arithmetic concepts.

Identifying and describing numeric and geometric patterns and making, testing, and applying generalizations about the data gathered from problem situations are the tools students use to develop algorithms and construct mathematical meaning.

Modeling is the process of taking a real-world problem, expressing it mathematically, finding a solution, and then interpreting the solution in the real-world context. It is the tool students use to connect mathematics to the real world. Examples of problems that are modeled include decision making, population growth, time/motion problems, games, and genetics.

Instructional Approach

The instructional approach in *Math Thematics* is designed to involve students in doing mathematics. They are actively engaged in:

- Investigating, discovering, and applying mathematics
- Using concrete materials to explore mathematical properties and relationships
- Working cooperatively
- Communicating their ideas orally and in writing
- Using technological tools when appropriate
- Integrating mathematical strands to solve real-world problems

Not all the instruction is through discovery learning. Direct instruction on concepts and skills is included when appropriate.

MIDDLE GRADES *Math Thematics*

Philosophy

The goal of the *Math Thematics* curriculum is to help all students develop their abilities to:

- Reason logically
- Apply mathematical skills to real-world activities
- Communicate about and through mathematics
- View mathematics as relevant to their lives and connected to other areas
- Understand the connections among the different strands of mathematics and the connections of mathematics to other content areas
- Feel confident in using quantitative and spatial information to make decisions
- Become independent learners with a desire for lifelong learning

Content

Math Thematics:

- Provides a complete 3-year mathematics curriculum for middle grades
- Implements the National Council of Teachers of Mathematics (NCTM) Curriculum and Evaluation Standards for Grades 5–8
- Is problem solving oriented
- Emphasizes critical thinking and reasoning over rote procedural drill
- Decreases the emphasis on review of "elementary" topics such as whole number computation
- Increases emphasis on data analysis and statistics, proportional reasoning, algebra, geometry, and discrete mathematics

Instructional Approach

The instructional approach is designed to get students involved in doing mathematics in a variety of settings. In *Math Thematics*, students are actively engaged in:

- Investigating, discovering, and applying mathematics
- Using concrete materials to explore mathematical properties and relationships
- Working cooperatively
- Communicating their ideas orally and in writing
- Using technological tools when appropriate
- Integrating mathematical strands to solve real-world problems

Not all the instruction is through discovery learning. Direct instruction of concepts and skills is included when appropriate. *Practice and Application, Spiral Review,* and *Extension* exercises reinforce and extend learning.

Organization of Material in Student Book

The mathematics content for each grade level is presented in one book containing eight thematic modules that connect the mathematical ideas to real-world applications.

This is Module 3 in Book 1. Each module should take about four weeks to complete.

Each module contains four to six sections, an *Extended Exploration*, a *Module Project,* and a *Review and Assessment.*

Module There are 8 modules in each book.

Section Each module has 4 to 6 sections. A section contains 1 to 3 explorations and requires 1 to 3 days to complete.

Exploration There are 1 to 3 explorations per section. Each exploration takes 1 day to complete.

Key Concepts The *Key Concepts* gives the main ideas and new terms of the section.

Practice & Application Exercises Homework exercises are assigned at the end of each exploration. *Practice & Application Exercises, Spiral Review,* and *Extension* reinforce and extend learning.

Extra Skill Practice The *Extra Skill Practice* provides additional exercises for students who need more practice.

4   MATH THEMATICS, Book 1

Module Themes and Content with NCTM Standards

Module 1: Tools for Success

Many of the approaches and tools of the program are introduced, including cooperative learning, using calculators, looking for patterns, and making connections. Problem solving is the focus, especially multiple strategies and ways to assess and improve problem solving. Estimation, mental math, basic geometric terms, and a review of whole number computation are woven throughout the module.

NUMBER *NCTM Standards 5, 6, and 7*
- whole number computation, estimation, and mental math
- decide when to use mental math, paper and pencil, or a calculator
- understand the order of operations

MEASUREMENT *NCTM Standard 13*

STATISTICS *NCTM Standard 10*

ALGEBRA *NCTM Standards 8 and 9*

GEOMETRY *NCTM Standards 12 and 13*
- identify basic geometric figures (lines, points, and so on)
- classify angles
- classify triangles by lengths of sides and angle measures
- recognize when three side lengths form a triangle

PROBABILITY *NCTM Standard 11*

DISCRETE MATH *NCTM Standard 8*
- identify and extend patterns
- write a rule to extend patterns
- use an ordered list to find all arrangements

Module 2: Patterns and Designs

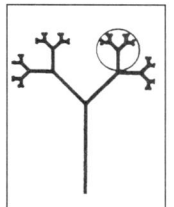

The mathematics of patterns and design is explored through such themes as kites, quilts, and automobile designs. Manipulatives and visual models are used to develop an understanding of geometry (shape classification and transformations) and number concepts (fraction and decimal representations). Students discover and analyze relationships and create their own patterns and designs.

NUMBER *NCTM Standards 5, 6, and 7*
- fraction, decimal, and mixed number concepts
- find equivalent fractions and fractions in lowest terms
- add and subtract decimals, plus estimation

MEASUREMENT *NCTM Standard 13*

STATISTICS *NCTM Standard 10*

ALGEBRA *NCTM Standards 8 and 9*

GEOMETRY *NCTM Standards 12 and 13*
- identify and classify polygons
- identify parallel lines and lines of symmetry
- identify congruent polygons
- perform transformations

PROBABILITY *NCTM Standard 11*

DISCRETE MATH *NCTM Standard 8*

PRESENTING

Professional Development Handbook

Module Themes and Content with NCTM Standards

Module 3: Statistical Safari

Data about animals are used to explore techniques for displaying information visually and analyzing it numerically. There are opportunities to apply written computation skills, develop mental math and estimation strategies, work with metric measurements, and use a calculator. Students focus on such themes as fish sampling, dinosaurs, and the work of wildlife biologists in managing sheep populations.

NUMBER *NCTM Standards 5, 6, and 7*
- find a fraction of a whole
- percent concepts
- fraction, decimal, and percent relationship
- decimal computation (rounding, division, estimation, and mental math)

MEASUREMENT *NCTM Standard 13*
- develop benchmarks to estimate metric length
- convert between metric units of length
- estimate metric mass
- convert between metric units of mass

STATISTICS *NCTM Standard 10*
- make predictions from a sample
- find the range of a set of data
- draw bar graphs, line plots, and stem-and-leaf plots
- find averages and determine which one is appropriate

ALGEBRA *NCTM Standards 8 and 9*

GEOMETRY *NCTM Standards 12 and 13*

PROBABILITY *NCTM Standard 11*

DISCRETE MATH *NCTM Standard 8*
- make and interpret Venn diagrams

Module 4: Mind Games

Students explore mathematical content by playing and analyzing strategy games. Topics studied include number theory, probability, fraction and decimal multiplication, an introduction to algebra, coordinate graphing, and hands-on work with mixed numbers. Winning strategies are developed through the use of tables, Venn diagrams, factor trees, and number sense.

NUMBER *NCTM Standards 5, 6, and 7*
- find factors, multiples, primes, and composites
- write numbers in exponential form
- multiply fractions and decimals, plus estimation
- mixed number concepts

MEASUREMENT *NCTM Standard 13*

STATISTICS *NCTM Standard 10*

ALGEBRA *NCTM Standards 8 and 9*
- graph ordered pairs in the first quadrant on a coordinate grid
- write and evaluate expressions and equations
- use tables, graphs, and equations to show relationships

GEOMETRY *NCTM Standards 12 and 13*
- find the area and perimeter of a rectangle

PROBABILITY *NCTM Standard 11*
- conduct an experiment
- find experimental and theoretical probabilities, and compare them
- identify impossible and certain events

DISCRETE MATH *NCTM Standard 8*

Module Themes and Content with NCTM Standards

Module 5: Creating Things

Themes such as mask design, origami, cooking, weaving, and geometric puzzle design are the settings for developing fraction operations using models, measurement, mental math, estimation, calculators, and written algorithms. Students also explore benchmarks and conversions for customary units of length and capacity.

NUMBER *NCTM Standards 5, 6, and 7*
- fraction and mixed number concepts
- add, subtract, multiply, and divide fractions and mixed numbers; use estimation and mental math
- use the distributive property

MEASUREMENT *NCTM Standard 13*
- develop benchmarks to estimate length and capacity in customary units
- convert between customary units of length
- convert between customary units of capacity

STATISTICS *NCTM Standard 10*

ALGEBRA *NCTM Standards 8 and 9*

GEOMETRY *NCTM Standards 12 and 13*

PROBABILITY *NCTM Standard 11*

DISCRETE MATH *NCTM Standard 8*

Module 6: Comparisons and Predictions

Situations from nature, literature, sports, and the news provide opportunities for students to build an understanding of ratios, proportions, and percent, and to solve problems involving comparisons and predictions. Models, graphs, tree diagrams, and tables are used to explore and represent relationships. Students also look at congruent and similar figures.

NUMBER *NCTM Standards 5, 6, and 7*
- ratio, rate, and proportion concepts
- fraction and percent relationship
- use mental math with fractions to find or estimate a percent of a number

MEASUREMENT *NCTM Standard 13*

STATISTICS *NCTM Standard 10*
- collect data
- create a scatter plot and draw a fitted line
- make predictions using a scatter plot

ALGEBRA *NCTM Standards 8 and 9*
- write a proportion with a variable
- use cross products to solve a proportion

GEOMETRY *NCTM Standards 12 and 13*
- identify similar and congruent figures
- apply similarity to solve problems involving scale drawings or models
- measure and draw angles

PROBABILITY *NCTM Standard 11*
- make a tree diagram to find probabilities
- understand the concept of a fair game

DISCRETE MATH *NCTM Standard 8*

Module Themes and Content with NCTM Standards

Module 7: Wonders of the World

An exploration of intriguing or impressive structures around the world leads to work with measurement and geometric figures, including the use of formulas. Themes include the Taj Mahal, the Great Pyramid, Mesa Verde, and the Empire State Building. Fraction and decimal computation skills are used to convert units and to find areas and volumes. Students also work with integers and coordinate graphs and solve equations.

NUMBER *NCTM Standards 5, 6, and 7*
- integer concepts
- compare integers

MEASUREMENT *NCTM Standard 13*
- estimate area and weight in customary units
- convert between units of area
- convert between customary units of weight
- use benchmarks to estimate temperature

STATISTICS *NCTM Standard 10*

ALGEBRA *NCTM Standards 8 and 9*
- write equations for area, volume, and circumference, and solve for a missing dimension
- find solutions for simple inequalities ($x < -3$)
- graph ordered pairs on a coordinate grid

GEOMETRY *NCTM Standards 12 and 13*
- find the areas of parallelograms, triangles, and circles
- recognize and make prisms, pyramids, and cylinders
- find the volumes of prisms and cylinders
- draw a circle, identify its parts, and find circumference

PROBABILITY *NCTM Standard 11*

DISCRETE MATH *NCTM Standard 8*

Module 8: Our Environment

Themes showing how the power of nature affects people and how people affect nature introduce integer addition and subtraction, scientific notation, metric capacity, and geometric probability. Topics investigated include lightning, population growth, and the supply of natural resources. Students also simulate a meteorite's fall to Earth and build on previous work with percent, volume, and misleading graphs and averages.

NUMBER *NCTM Standards 5, 6, and 7*
- add and subtract integers
- write numbers in scientific notation
- use a decimal to find a percent of a number
- understand percents greater than 100%

MEASUREMENT *NCTM Standard 13*
- understand the relationship between volume and capacity in the metric system
- estimate capacity in metric units
- convert between metric units of capacity

STATISTICS *NCTM Standard 10*
- interpret and make graphs, including line graphs and circle graphs
- recognize misleading graphs and averages
- choose an appropriate graph or average

ALGEBRA *NCTM Standards 8 and 9*

GEOMETRY *NCTM Standards 12 and 13*

PROBABILITY *NCTM Standard 11*
- conduct an experiment
- find geometric probability
- use probability to make predictions

DISCRETE MATH *NCTM Standard 8*

8   *Math Thematics*, Book 1

MIDDLE GRADES *Math Thematics*

Why Change Mathematics Education?

> Mathematics is the key to opportunity. No longer just the language of science, mathematics now contributes in direct and fundamental ways to business, finance, health, and defense. For students, it opens doors to careers. For citizens, it enables informed decisions. For nations, it provides knowledge to compete in a technological economy. To participate fully in the world of the future, America must tap the power of mathematics.
>
> — *Everybody Counts* (1989)

The needs of industry, low test scores, and research on how students learn all contribute to the need to change mathematics education.

Industry

It has been estimated that the amount spent on mathematics education in the U.S. is about $25 billion per year. In addition, industry spends an equivalent amount on remedial mathematics education for employees. (*Everybody Counts*, 1989)

Businesses need employees who can solve problems, communicate, and work in teams and alone. Simply knowing the "basics" is not enough given the growing use of technology and the higher level thinking required for many jobs. (*NCTM 1997–98 Handbook*)

Test Scores

The most recent international test of mathematical knowledge of 8th grade students (TIMSS), shows that 20 countries outperform U.S. students, while U.S. students outperform their counterparts in only 7 nations. (*Pursuing Excellence*, 1996)

Learning Mathematics

Students best learn mathematics when they go through the process of constructing it. Instead of memorizing rules or algorithms, students should discover math content through experiments, games, or other activities. (*Breaking the Barriers*, 1992)

Professional Development Handbook

EXPLORING Math Thematics, Book 1

Close-Up of a Section

To understand the structure of *Math Thematics,* we'll look closely at a section in Module 3 of Book 1. In *Dinosaurs,* students investigate the sizes of dinosaurs and how much they ate, motivating the exploration of stem-and-leaf plots and the discovery of how to divide by a decimal.

Dinosaurs is the last section of a module centered around animals. In previous modules and in earlier sections of this module, students have:

- Extended patterns and analyzed sequences
- Examined and classified triangles and other polygons
- Learned the 4-step approach to solving problems
- Used estimation, mental math, and a calculator to explore appropriate tools for computation
- Investigated order of operations
- Investigated fraction, mixed number, percent, and decimal concepts
- Added and subtracted decimals
- Created and interpreted bar graphs and line plots
- Found the mean, the median, and the mode of a data set
- Learned to divide a decimal by a whole number

Organization of a Section

Each section contains:

SETTING THE STAGE & THINK ABOUT IT QUESTIONS

ONE OR MORE EXPLORATIONS

KEY CONCEPTS & QUESTIONS

PRACTICE & APPLICATION EXERCISES

EXTRA SKILL PRACTICE

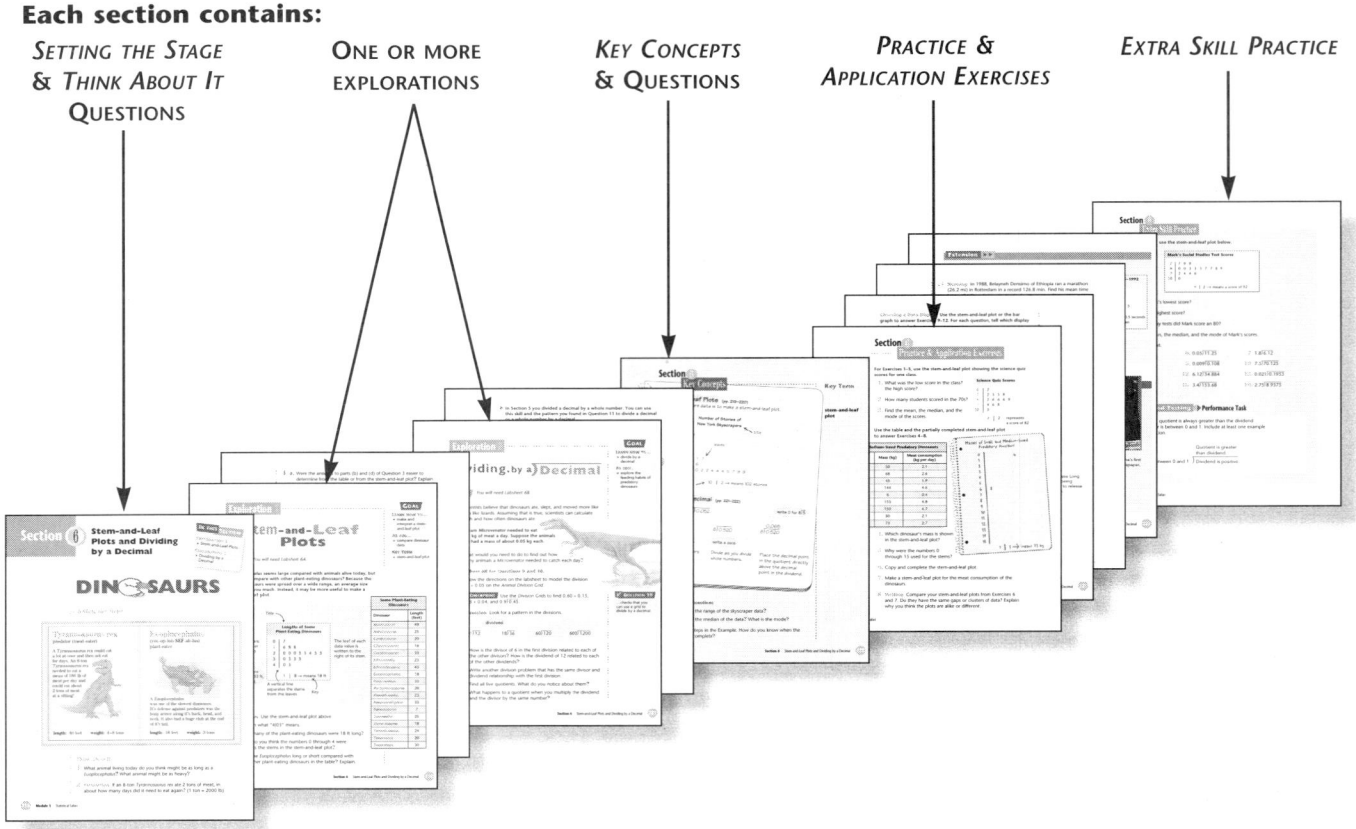

Section 6: Stem-and-Leaf Plots and Dividing by a Decimal

IN THIS SECTION
- EXPLORATION 1 ♦ Stem-and-Leaf Plots
- EXPLORATION 2 ♦ Dividing by a Decimal

DINOSAURS

Setting the Stage

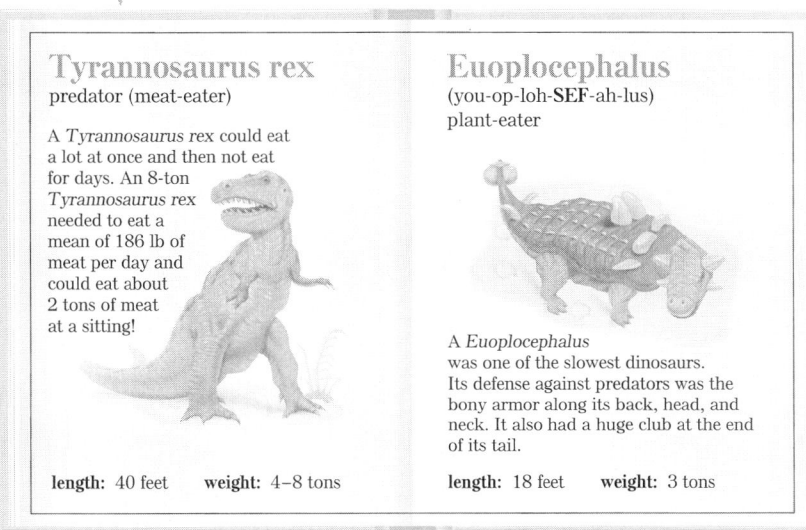

Tyrannosaurus rex
predator (meat-eater)

A *Tyrannosaurus rex* could eat a lot at once and then not eat for days. An 8-ton *Tyrannosaurus rex* needed to eat a mean of 186 lb of meat per day and could eat about 2 tons of meat at a sitting!

length: 40 feet **weight:** 4–8 tons

Euoplocephalus
(you-op-loh-**SEF**-ah-lus)
plant-eater

A *Euoplocephalus* was one of the slowest dinosaurs. Its defense against predators was the bony armor along its back, head, and neck. It also had a huge club at the end of its tail.

length: 18 feet **weight:** 3 tons

Think About It

1. What animal living today do you think might be as long as a *Euoplocephalus*? What animal might be as heavy?

2. **Estimation** If an 8-ton *Tyrannosaurus rex* ate 2 tons of meat, in about how many days did it need to eat again? (1 ton = 2000 lb)

Module 3 Statistical Safari

Introduction to Setting the Stage

The purpose of the *Setting the Stage* is to pique students' interest and relate the mathematics to a real-world situation. This is an integral part of a section since it provides the motivation for learning the mathematics or introduces the problem that will be explored. The *Setting the Stage* may be a reading, activity, visual display, or some combination of these. Students may review a previously learned concept in the *Think About It* questions, but usually they intuitively explore an idea that they will later investigate in depth. Mental math and estimation are often incorporated into the *Think About It* questions.

EXPLORING

Reflecting Questions on the Setting the Stage

A. This module contains six sections, but this is the only one about dinosaurs. What other animals do you think students would find interesting? Is there one animal topic that would appeal to all students? Explain.

B. **Discussion** What is a follow-up question you could ask students after Question 2 in the *Think About It*?

Professional Development Handbook

Statistics Strand in Math Thematics

We are confronted with statistics in our everyday lives. Newspapers, magazines, and television use statistical displays and averages to communicate about social, economic, political, and educational concerns. Students will need to be able to analyze these claims and displays to make informed decisions.

Statistics, the science of data, has blossomed from roots in agriculture and genetics into a rich mathematical science that provides essential tools both for analyses of uncertainty and for forecasts of future events. From clinical research to market surveys, from enhancement of digital photographs to stock market models, statistical methods permeate policy analysis in every area of human affairs.

—*Everybody Counts, 1989*

Throughout the three books of *Math Thematics*, statistics is a vital and recurring strand. This spiraling process strengthens students' understanding of the content by providing different contexts for the statistical displays and analyses. The chart below shows the first exposure to various statistical concepts at each grade level. For example, stem-and-leaf plots are first introduced in Module 3 of Book 1. In Books 2 and 3, students analyze and create these plots in the context of running times and musical achievement, and then continue using stem-and-leaf plots throughout the later modules of each book.

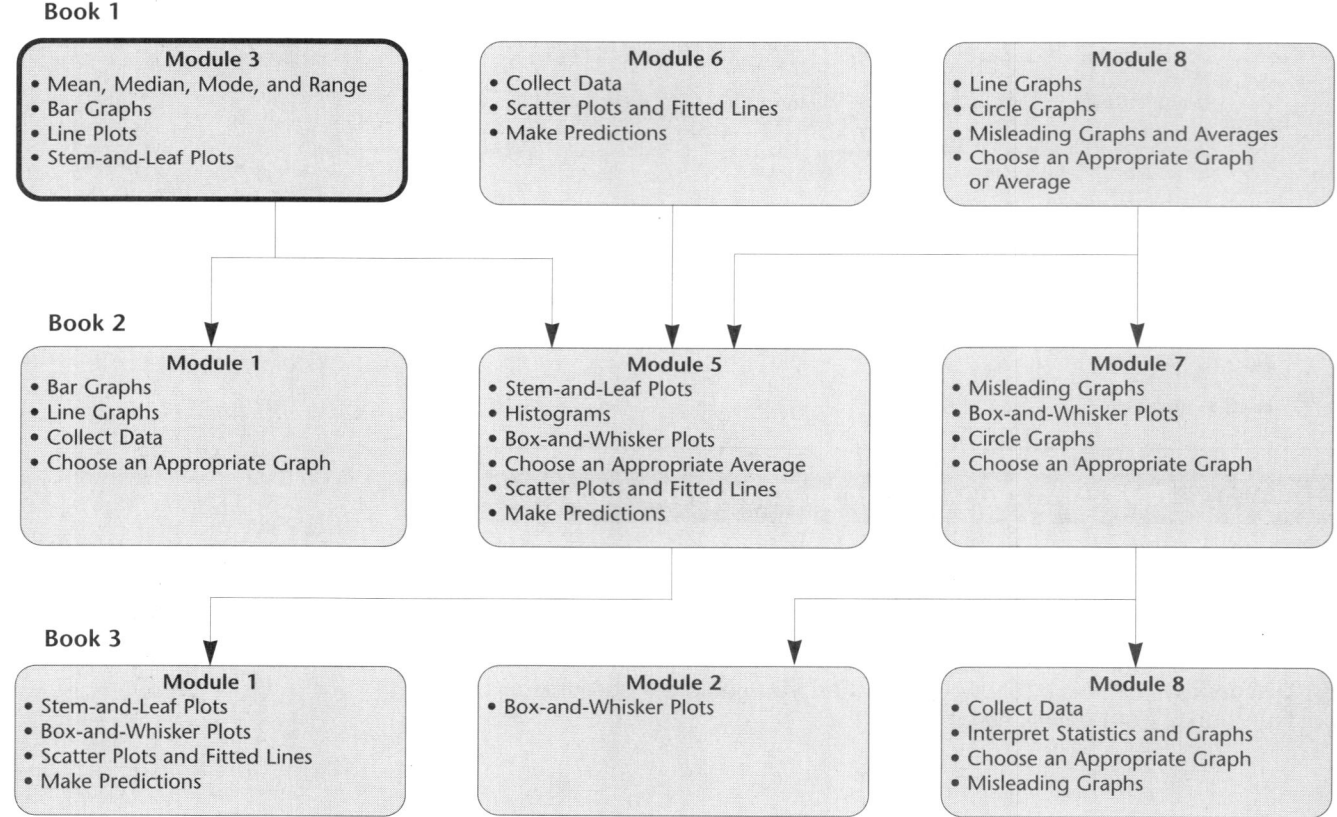

Book 1

Module 3
- Mean, Median, Mode, and Range
- Bar Graphs
- Line Plots
- Stem-and-Leaf Plots

Module 6
- Collect Data
- Scatter Plots and Fitted Lines
- Make Predictions

Module 8
- Line Graphs
- Circle Graphs
- Misleading Graphs and Averages
- Choose an Appropriate Graph or Average

Book 2

Module 1
- Bar Graphs
- Line Graphs
- Collect Data
- Choose an Appropriate Graph

Module 5
- Stem-and-Leaf Plots
- Histograms
- Box-and-Whisker Plots
- Choose an Appropriate Average
- Scatter Plots and Fitted Lines
- Make Predictions

Module 7
- Misleading Graphs
- Box-and-Whisker Plots
- Circle Graphs
- Choose an Appropriate Graph

Book 3

Module 1
- Stem-and-Leaf Plots
- Box-and-Whisker Plots
- Scatter Plots and Fitted Lines
- Make Predictions

Module 2
- Box-and-Whisker Plots

Module 8
- Collect Data
- Interpret Statistics and Graphs
- Choose an Appropriate Graph
- Misleading Graphs

Exploration 1

Stem-and-Leaf Plots

SET UP You will need Labsheet 6A.

GOAL

LEARN HOW TO...
- make and interpret a stem-and-leaf plot

AS YOU...
- compare dinosaur data

KEY TERM
- stem-and-leaf plot

▶ A *Euoplocephalus* seems large compared with animals alive today, but how did it compare with other plant-eating dinosaurs? Because the sizes of dinosaurs were spread over a wide range, an average size may not tell you much. Instead, it may be more useful to make a **stem-and-leaf plot**.

Lengths of Some Plant-Eating Dinosaurs ← Title

```
0 | 7
1 | 6 8 8
2 | 0 0 0 3 3 4 5 5
3 | 0 3 3 3
4 | 0 3
```

The stems are listed in order from least to greatest.

The leaf of each data value is written to the right of its stem.

This row contains the lengths 30 ft, 33 ft, 33 ft, and 33 ft.

A vertical line separates the stems from the leaves.

1 | 8 → means 18 ft   Key

Some Plant-Eating Dinosaurs	
Dinosaur	Length (feet)
Anatosaurus	40
Ankylosaurus	25
Centrosaurus	20
Chasmosaurus	16
Corythosaurus	33
Edmontonia	23
Edmontosaurus	43
Euoplocephalus	18
Hadrosaurus	33
Pachyrhinosaurus	20
Panoplosaurus	23
Parasaurolophus	33
Parksosaurus	7
Sauropelta	25
Styracosaurus	18
Tenontosaurus	24
Torosaurus	20
Triceratops	30

3 **Discussion** Use the stem-and-leaf plot above.

a. Explain what "4|03" means.

b. How many of the plant-eating dinosaurs were 18 ft long?

c. Why do you think the numbers 0 through 4 were used as the stems in the stem-and-leaf plot?

d. Was the *Euoplocephalus* long or short compared with the other plant-eating dinosaurs in the table? Explain.

Section 6 Stem-and-Leaf Plots and Dividing by a Decimal 219

Introduction to an Exploration

After the *Setting the Stage*, each section contains one to three explorations where students are actively involved in learning new mathematical content. Each exploration requires one class period, and, depending on the nature of the activity, may be completed by students working individually, in small groups, or as a whole class. The activities in the explorations range from guided discovery to open-ended investigations. Many involve the use of concrete, hands-on materials. In an exploration, students investigate a question or problem by doing one or more of the following:

- Collecting, generating, researching, and presenting data
- Using concrete and/or visual models
- Applying problem-solving strategies
- Looking for patterns and relations
- Exploring alternative methods and solutions
- Using number sense
- Applying prior knowledge

The explorations provide opportunities for students to observe, analyze, predict, make and test conjectures, draw conclusions, and communicate their ideas orally and in writing.

Professional Development Handbook

4. **a.** Were the answers to parts (b) and (d) of Question 3 easier to determine from the table or from the stem-and-leaf plot? Explain.

   b. What information from the table do you lose by showing the data in a stem-and-leaf plot?

Use Labsheet 6A for Questions 5 and 6.

5. **Try This as a Class** Follow the directions on the labsheet to complete the stem-and-leaf plot for the *Weights of Plant-Eating Dinosaurs*.

6. Look at your stem-and-leaf plot from Question 5.

   a. Why is there no leaf for the stem 1?

   b. What are the modes of the plant-eating dinosaur weights? What is the median?

   c. How did the weight of a *Euoplocephalus* compare with the weights of the other plant-eating dinosaurs in the table?

   d. How are the stem-and-leaf plots for the weights and lengths of the plant-eating dinosaurs similar? How are they different?

▶ A stem-and-leaf plot can also be used to compare the lengths of predatory dinosaurs with the lengths of the plant-eating dinosaurs they ate.

Some Predatory Dinosaurs

Dinosaur	Length (feet)
Albertosaurus	26
Allosaurus	35
Chirostenotes	7
Daspletosaurus	30
Deinonychus	13
Dromaeosaurus	6
Dromiceiomimus	11
Microvenator	4
Nanotyrannous	17
Ornithomimus	13
Struthiomimus	13
Troödon	8
Tyrannosaurus rex	40
Velociraptor	7

✓ QUESTION 7

…checks that you can make and interpret a stem-and-leaf plot.

7. **✓ CHECKPOINT** Make a stem-and-leaf plot for the lengths of the predatory dinosaurs in the table.

   a. How did an 18-foot-long *Euoplocephalus* compare in length with the predatory dinosaurs?

   b. Use your stem-and-leaf plot and the one on page 219. How did the lengths of the plant-eating dinosaurs compare with the lengths of the predatory dinosaurs?

HOMEWORK EXERCISES ▶ See Exs. 1–12 on pp. 224–225.

Module 3 Statistical Safari

Math Thematics, Book 1

Labsheets

Labsheets for *Math Thematics* are blacklines provided in the *Teacher's Resource Book*.

Name _____ Date _____

MODULE 3 **LABSHEET 6A**

Weights of Plant-Eating Dinosaurs
(Use with Questions 5 and 6 on page 220.)

Directions Complete parts (a)–(d) to make a stem-and-leaf plot for the weights of the plant-eating dinosaurs listed in the table.

a. Find the least and the greatest data items in the table to help you choose the stem numbers. List each stem in a column from least to greatest on the blank stem-and-leaf plot below.

b. In the table, place a check next to the data that have a stem of 3. Use your list to write the leaves for the stem 3 in order from least to greatest in the stem-and-leaf plot below. Do this for each stem using a different mark or color.

c. Fill in the key so that it tells the values represented by a stem and leaf.

d. Write a title for the stem-and-leaf plot so that anyone can tell what it is about.

Some Plant-Eating Dinosaurs

Dinosaur	Weight (tons)
Anatosaurus	3.5
Ankylosaurus	5.0
Centrosaurus	2.6
Chasmosaurus	2.2
Corythosaurus	3.7
Edmontonia	3.9
Edmontosaurus	3.9
Euoplocephalus	3.0
Hadrosaurus	3.0
Pachyrhinosaurus	4.0
Panoplosaurus	4.0
Parasaurolophus	3.5
Parksosaurus	0.1
Sauropelta	2.7
Styracosaurus	2.7
Tenontosaurus	2.0
Torosaurus	5.0
Triceratops	5.3

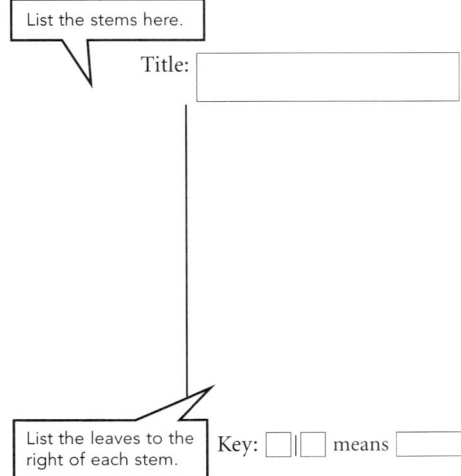

Title: _____

Key: ☐ | ☐ means _____

Copyright © by McDougal Littell Inc. All rights reserved.

Math Thematics, Book 1 **3-63**

Reflecting Questions on Exploration 1

Use student pages 219, 220, and Labsheet 6A (pp. 13–15 of this handbook).

C. **Discussion** Look at the *Goal, Key Term,* and *Set Up* on page 219.
   - Which should students read?
   - Which can help you, as the teacher, with classroom management?

D. To better understand the process students will go through, use the student pages to complete Exploration 1.

E. Archeologists have categorized dinosaur lengths as small, medium, and large.
   - Based on the stem-and-leaf plot on page 219, what size best describes the *Euoplocephalus*? Why?
   - Based on your stem-and-leaf plot for Question 7 on page 220, what size best describes the *Tyrannosaurus rex*? Why?

Most of the *Math Thematics* materials are written so that students discover the mathematics. Through the use of manipulatives, models, and hands-on activities, students actively learn the concepts. The rules and algorithms usually associated with mathematics are student-derived, rather than given in the text. Since some concepts or applications do not lend themselves to discovery learning, direct instruction is also used in *Math Thematics*.

F. **Discussion**
   - What process do students go through to learn how to make a stem-and-leaf plot?
   - How is the teacher involved in this process?

G. **Try This as a Class** Question 5 is titled *Try This as a Class*. The class may be brought together for a variety of reasons.
   - Why do you think the class was brought together for Question 5?
   - Are there other situations in which you would bring your class together to answer a question? Explain.

Number Strand in Math Thematics

Number includes the concepts and skills associated with understanding and representing numbers, using the place-value system, and performing operations. Number sense and estimation are important components of the number strand and appear throughout *Math Thematics*. The learner outcomes for this strand are:

- Students should be able to apply number theory concepts.

- Students should be able to represent, use, and have a sense of rational and irrational numbers in real-world problem situations.

- Students should be able to demonstrate operations, order relations, and number sense for rational and irrational numbers.

- Students should be able to apply proportional reasoning in problem solving and in discovering mathematical concepts.

Number concepts, such as computation, mental math, and estimation, are explored throughout Book 1 of *Math Thematics*. Students see many of the number ideas in Modules 1, 2, 3, 4, 5, and 7 of Book 2, but by the time they reach Book 3, most elementary number concepts are assumed. The chart at the right shows the development of number in all three books.

Book 1

Module 1
- Whole Number Computation, Estimation, and Mental Math
- Order of Operations

Module 2
- Fraction, Decimal, and Mixed Number Concepts
- Add and Subtract Decimals*
- Equivalent Fractions

Module 3
- Percent Concepts
- Fraction, Decimal, and Percent Relationship
- Divide Decimals

Module 4
- Factors, Multiples, Primes, and Composites
- Exponential Form
- Multiply Fractions and Decimals*
- Mixed Number Concepts

Module 5
- Fraction and Mixed Number Concepts
- Add, Subtract, Multiply, and Divide Fractions and Mixed Numbers*

Module 6
- Ratio, Rate, and Proportion Concepts
- Estimate Percents Using Fractions

Module 7
- Comparing Integers

Module 8
- Add and Subtract Integers
- Scientific Notation
- Multiply by a Decimal to Find a Percent of a Number
- Percents Greater Than 100%

Book 2

Module 1
- Percent and Exponent Concepts Review
- Order of Operations

Module 2
- Compare Integers
- Opposite and Absolute Value
- Add and Subtract Integers
- Properties of Addition

Module 3
- Factors, Multiples, Primes, and Composites
- Add and Subtract Fractions and Mixed Numbers*
- Scientific Notation

Module 4
- Multiply and Divide Fractions, Mixed Numbers, Decimals, and Integers*
- Reciprocals

Module 5
- Ratio, Rate, and Proportion Concepts
- Find Percents
- Fraction, Decimal, and Percent Relationship

Module 6
- Inequalities
- Approximate and Find Square Roots
- Write Proportions in Context

Module 7
- Percent Greater than 100%*
- Percents less than 1%
- Percent of Change

Book 3

Module 1
- Rate, Ratio, and Exponent Review*

Module 2
- Solve Proportions
- Find Percents and Percent of Change
- Add, Subtract, Multiply, and Divide Integers

Module 3
- Approximate and Find Square Roots
- Order of Operations
- Scientific Notation

Module 4
- Multiply and Divide Rational Numbers

Module 5
- Zero and Negative Exponents
- Scientific Notation
- Properties of Exponents

Module 6
- Ratio Applications
- Inequalities

* includes mental math and estimation

Professional Development Handbook

Exploration 2

Dividing by a Decimal

GOAL

LEARN HOW TO...
• divide by a decimal

AS YOU...
• explore the feeding habits of predatory dinosaurs

SET UP You will need Labsheet 6B.

Some scientists believe that dinosaurs ate, slept, and moved more like birds than like lizards. Assuming that is true, scientists can calculate how much and how often dinosaurs ate.

▶ A 6-kilogram *Microvenator* needed to eat about 0.4 kg of meat a day. Suppose the animals it hunted had a mass of about 0.05 kg each.

8 What would you need to do to find out how many animals a *Microvenator* needed to catch each day?

Use Labsheet 6B for Questions 9 and 10.

9 Follow the directions on the labsheet to model the division 0.4 ÷ 0.05 on the *Animal Division Grid*.

10 ✓ **CHECKPOINT** Use the *Division Grids* to find 0.60 ÷ 0.15, 0.28 ÷ 0.04, and $0.9\overline{)0.45}$.

✓ **QUESTION 10**
...checks that you can use a grid to divide by a decimal.

11 Discussion Look for a pattern in the divisions.

divisor   dividend

$6\overline{)12}$ $18\overline{)36}$ $60\overline{)120}$ $600\overline{)1200}$

a. How is the divisor of 6 in the first division related to each of the other divisors? How is the dividend of 12 related to each of the other dividends?

b. Write another division problem that has the same divisor and dividend relationship with the first division.

c. Find all five quotients. What do you notice about them?

d. What happens to a quotient when you multiply the dividend and the divisor by the same number?

Section 6 Stem-and-Leaf Plots and Dividing by a Decimal   **221**

Math Thematics, Book 1

Name _____ Date _____

MODULE 3 **LABSHEET 6B**

Animal Division Grid (Use with Question 9 on page 221.)

Directions Complete parts (a)–(e) to divide 0.4 by 0.05.

A 6-kilogram *Microvenator* needed to eat about 0.4 kg of meat a day. Suppose the animals it hunted had a mass of about 0.05 kg each. To find how many animals a *Microvenator* needed to catch each day, you need to divide 0.4 by 0.05.

You can use a 10 × 10 grid to model the division. Let the grid represent one unit.

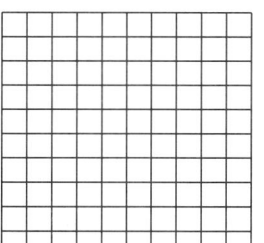

a. Shade 0.4 of the grid.

b. Divide the shaded area into equal-sized groups with 0.05 in each group.

c. How many equal-sized groups are there?

d. 0.4 ÷ 0.05 = ____

e. How many animals did a Microvenator need to catch each day?

Division Grids (Use with Question 10 on page 221.)

Directions Use each grid to find the quotient.

a. 0.60 ÷ 0.15 = ____   b. 0.28 ÷ 0.04 = ____   c. 0.9)‾0.45 = ____   [0.45 ÷ 0.9]

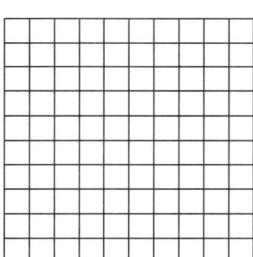 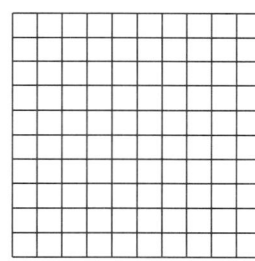 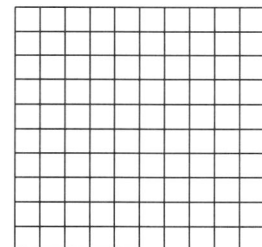

▶ In Section 5 you divided a decimal by a whole number. You can use this skill and the pattern you found in Question 11 to divide a decimal or a whole number by a decimal.

12 A 68-kilogram *Deinonychus* needed to eat a mean of about 2.6 kg of meat per day. Suppose a *Deinonychus* ate 12.48 kg of a *Hadrosaurus* all at once. To find out in how many days it needed to eat again, you can do this division:

$$2.6 \overline{)12.48}$$

   a. What can 2.6 be multiplied by to make it a whole number?

   b. If you multiply the divisor by the number you found in part (a), what must you do to the dividend to keep the quotient from changing?

   c. Rewrite the division by performing the operations described in parts (a) and (b). Then find the quotient. In how many days did the *Deinonychus* need to eat again?

13 Discussion To find the quotient $0.25 \overline{)28}$, Roland rewrote the division as $25 \overline{)280}$. Is this correct? Explain.

✓ **QUESTION 14**
...checks that you can divide by a decimal.

14 ✓ **CHECKPOINT** Find each quotient.

   a. $0.9 \overline{)0.072}$ **b.** $0.426 \div 0.12$ **c.** $2.4 \overline{)9}$

15 A *Velociraptor* had a mass of about 70 kg and ate about one fourth of its own body weight of meat at one sitting.

   a. How much would a *Velociraptor* eat at one sitting?

   b. Suppose a pack of *Velociraptors* hunted a 448-kilogram *Tenontosaur*. About how many *Velociraptors* could the *Tenontosaur* feed?

HOMEWORK EXERCISES ▶ See Exs. 13–26 on pp. 225–226.

222 **Module 3** Statistical Safari

Reflecting Questions on Exploration 2

Use student pages 221, 222, and Labsheet 6B (pp. 18–20 of this handbook).

H. Read over the introductory paragraphs and Question 8 at the beginning of Exploration 2. What "problem" are students trying to solve?

I. Students use a model in Questions 9 and 10 to divide by a decimal. Is a model used for the rest of the exploration? If not, what learning technique is used?

J. How does Question 9 help students conceptualize division with decimals?

K. With a partner, complete Questions 11, 12, and 15.

L. Both Questions 10 and 14 are *Checkpoints*. *Checkpoints* are a way to quickly assess whether students understand the mathematics.

- What does Question 10 assess? Question 14?

- **Discussion** What would you do if students understood and could answer Question 10 correctly but had difficulty with Question 14?

M. **Discussion**

- *Discussion* questions can be explored in pairs, groups of four, or as a class. Look at the two *Discussion* questions in Exploration 2 (Questions 11 and 13). What group size would you use to talk about each of them? What factors would influence your decision?

- *Discussion* questions are one place where students communicate about mathematics. At what other points in an exploration do students communicate about mathematics? Is the communication always in an oral format? Explain.

Introduction to Key Concepts

Students can use the *Key Concepts* to review for a test or as a reference when they have missed a day of class. The *Key Concepts* are also a resource for parents who are helping their child with homework. These pages give a quick overview of the content, illustrate the content with examples, highlight the most important content, and provide a reference to the applicable pages in the explorations. The *Key Concepts* questions reinforce the ideas from the section.

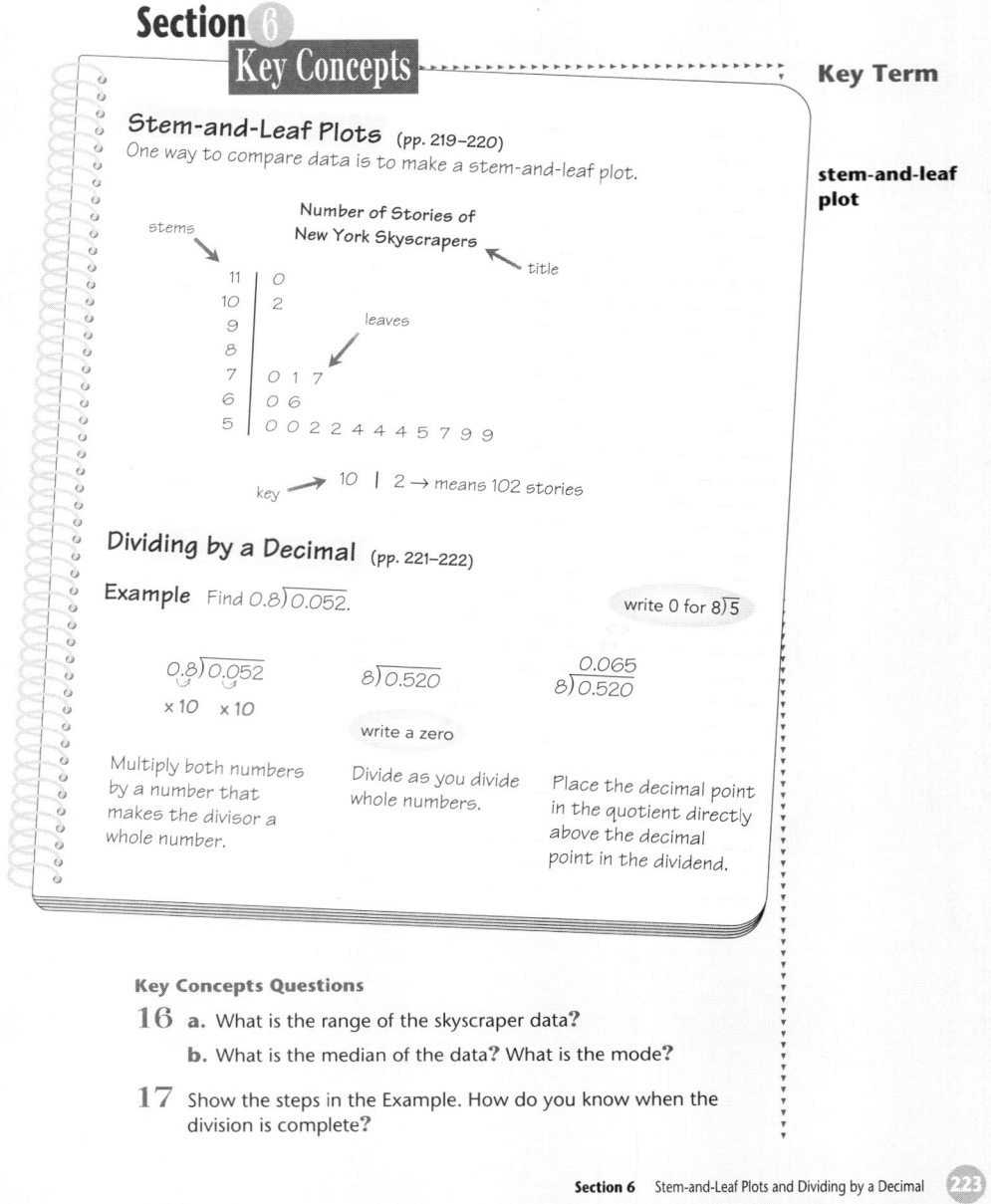

Reflecting Questions on the Key Concepts

N. • Complete Question 16.

• How does Question 16 help reinforce the ideas presented in the explorations?

• How does this question help students understand why you might want to use a stem-and-leaf plot?

O. Students never formally describe a rule for dividing by a decimal. How does Question 17 help students further clarify the steps for dividing by a decimal?

Section 6
Practice & Application Exercises

For Exercises 1–3, use the stem-and-leaf plot showing the science quiz scores for one class.

1. What was the low score in the class? the high score?

2. How many students scored in the 70s?

3. Find the mean, the median, and the mode of the scores.

Science Quiz Scores

```
 6 | 2
 7 | 2 3 5 8
 8 | 2 6 6 6 9
 9 | 4 6 8
10 | 0
```

8 | 2 represents a score of 82

Use the table and the partially completed stem-and-leaf plot to answer Exercises 4–8.

Small and Medium-Sized Predatory Dinosaurs

Dinosaur	Mass (kg)	Meat consumption (kg per day)
Chirostenotes	50	2.1
Deinonychus	68	2.6
Dromaeosaurus	45	1.9
Dromiceiomimus	144	4.6
Microvenator	6	0.4
Ornithomimus	153	4.8
Struthiomimus	150	4.7
Troödon	50	2.1
Velociraptor	73	2.7

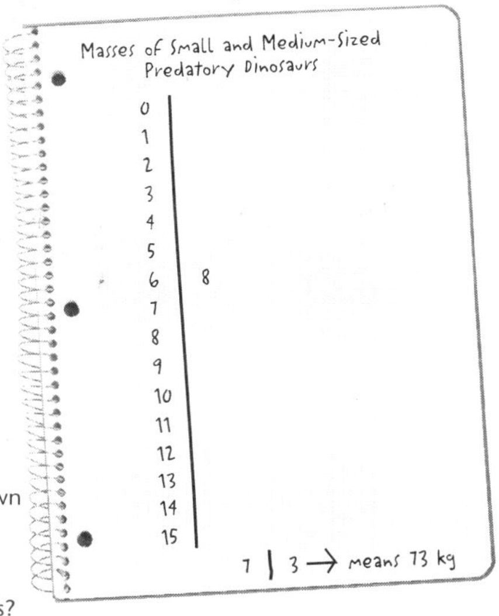

Masses of Small and Medium-Sized Predatory Dinosaurs

```
 0 |
 1 |
 2 |
 3 |
 4 |
 5 |
 6 | 8
 7 |
 8 |
 9 |
10 |
11 |
12 |
13 |
14 |
15 |
```

7 | 3 → means 73 kg

4. Which dinosaur's mass is shown in the stem-and-leaf plot?

5. Why were the numbers 0 through 15 used for the stems?

6. Copy and complete the stem-and-leaf plot.

7. Make a stem-and-leaf plot for the meat consumption of the dinosaurs.

8. **Writing** Compare your stem-and-leaf plots from Exercises 6 and 7. Do they have the same gaps or clusters of data? Explain why you think the plots are alike or different.

Module 3 Statistical Safari

Introduction to Practice & Application Exercises

The questions in the *Practice & Application Exercises* range from skill level to application and open-ended to single answer. There are a wide variety of topics covered in these exercises. Students may explore how the content relates to other areas of mathematics, other subjects, or different cultures. The exercises were written to assess how well students comprehend the content. The *Teacher's Resource Book* provides a guide to using the embedded assessment items and the *Reflecting on the Section* exercise to assess student learning.

EXPLORING

Choosing a Data Display Use the stem-and-leaf plot or the bar graph to answer Exercises 9–12. For each question, tell which display you used and why.

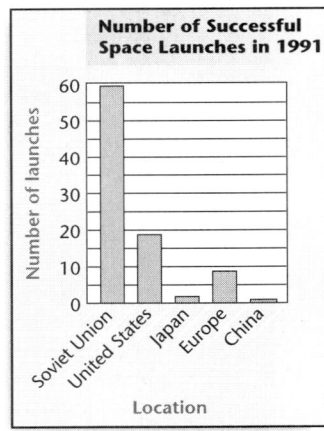

◄ The Chinese Long March 2 being launched to release a satellite.

9. Which location had 18 space launches in 1991?

10. What was the greatest number of launches for a location?

11. Which location had the least number of space launches?

12. What was the total number of space launches in 1991?

Find each quotient. Show your work.

13. $0.07 \overline{)4.2}$
14. $3 \overline{)0.06}$
15. $0.3 \overline{)0.84}$
16. $0.5 \overline{)0.356}$
17. $2.4 \overline{)45}$
18. $0.8 \overline{)4.9}$
19. $0.002 \overline{)0.571}$
20. $7.5 \overline{)16.2}$
21. $6.25 \overline{)5.6375}$

22. Apples are on sale for $.48 per pound. How many pounds of apples can you buy for $3?

23. The height of a tree is 542.85 cm. In a photograph of the tree, the height is only 0.7 cm. The tree's actual height is how many times as large as its height in the photo?

Section 6 Stem-and-Leaf Plots and Dividing by a Decimal

24. **Running** In 1988, Belayneh Densimo of Ethiopia ran a marathon (26.2 mi) in Rotterdam in a record 126.8 min. Find his mean time for a mile. Round your answer to the nearest tenth.

25. **Challenge** A carpenter is cutting a board that is 3.75 m long into pieces that are 0.3 m long. How many pieces can the carpenter cut from the board? How long is the leftover piece of board?

> **Journal**
> Exercise 26 checks that you can interpret a stem-and-leaf plot and can divide by a decimal.

Reflecting on the Section

Write your response to Exercise 26 in your journal.

Weights of Selected Newborns

```
6 | 3 4
7 | 2 2 4
8 | 0 3
9 | 2

7 | 2 → means 7.2 lb
```

Weights of Selected 1-Year-Olds

```
1 | 7 8 8 8 9
2 | 3 5
3 | 0

2 | 3 → means 23 lb
```

26. Use the stem-and-leaf plots above.

   a. Find the mean weight for newborns and for 1-year-olds.

   b. A 1-year-old is about how many times as heavy as a newborn? (Use the mean weights from part (a).)

   c. Can you tell what the 1-year-old weight is for a 9.2 lb newborn? Explain.

Spiral Review

Estimation Use front-end estimation to estimate each sum. (Module 3, p. 213)

27. 1250 + 3782   28. 16.7 + 4.8 + 5.4   29. 820 + 345 + 521

Is each figure a polygon? If not, explain why not. (Module 2, p. 87)

30.    31.    32.    33.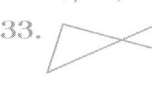

Write each fraction as a percent. (Module 3, p. 176)

34. $\frac{4}{5}$ 35. $\frac{6}{20}$ 36. $\frac{1}{4}$ 37. $\frac{3}{25}$

The *Extension* extends the ideas of the section to provide an additional challenge for some students.

Extension ▶▶

Back-to-Back Stem-and-Leaf Plots

You can use a *back-to-back stem-and-leaf plot* to compare two related sets of data.

Olympic 100-Meter Dash Winning Times 1956–1992 (to the nearest tenth of a second)

Men		Women
9 9	9	
5 3 2 1 1 0 0 0	10	5 8
	11	0 0 0 1 1 1 4 5

means 10.0 seconds for men ← 0 | 10 | 5 → means 10.5 seconds for women

38. What is the fastest time for a man? for a woman?

39. Find the mean, the median, and the modes for each set of data.

40. What time did both a man and a woman get?

41. Why does a back-to-back stem-and-leaf plot make it easy to compare the data sets?

The *Career Connection* features a person who uses the math ideas of the section in his or her job.

Career Connection

Publisher: Lizette Cruz-Watko

Newspaper publishers like Lizette Cruz-Watko use a unit called a *column inch* to measure the height and width of newspaper text. In Lizette's newspaper one column inch is 2.065 in. wide. Blank space is left between column inches.

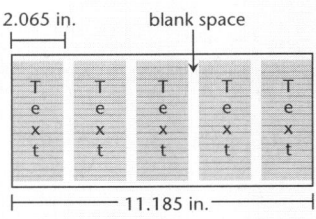

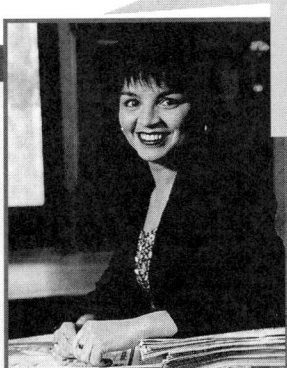

▲ Lizette Cruz-Watko launched North Carolina's first Spanish-language newspaper, *La Voz de Carolina*.

42. Lizette's newspaper is 11.185 in. wide and 5 column inches across as shown above. How many inches are left for the blank space between the columns of text?

43. Use your answer to Exercise 42 to find how many inches apart the columns of text are in the newspaper.

Section 6 Stem-and-Leaf Plots and Dividing by a Decimal 227

EXPLORING

Reflecting Questions on the *Practice & Application Exercises*

Use student pages 224–227 (pp. 23–26 of this handbook).

P. Try This as a Class The homework exercises for Exploration 1 are Exercises 1–12.

- Where in the section are the homework exercises identified?
- Which exercises repeat some of the development in the exploration?
- Which exercises extend the ideas in the exploration?

Q. Exercises 13, 17, 19, 23, and 24 are embedded assessment items for dividing by a decimal. Why do you think these exercises were chosen?

R. Why do you think Exercise 25 is a *Challenge* problem?

S. How does the *Reflecting on the Section* question (Exercise 26) help students see the connections between the statistics and number strands? What other ideas do students explore in this exercise?

Exercises 38–41 are part of the *Extension*. Every module contains at least one *Extension*. Although *Extensions* were written to accommodate advanced learners, many of them can be used as a class or group exploration.

T. Discussion Read over the *Extension* on page 227. Why might students have trouble reading a back-to-back stem-and-leaf plot?

The *Career Connections* are application-based exercises that can be assigned to all students.

U. What math concepts are needed to complete Exercises 42 and 43?

Introduction to Extra Skill Practice

The first half of the *Extra Skill Practice* reinforces the concepts students investigated in the section. The exercises are usually at a skill level but sometimes are application-based.

The bottom half of the page focuses on *Study Skills* in the first section and *Standardized Testing* in all other sections. The *Study Skills* questions explore how students learn (visual, auditory, or kinesthetic), how to take notes, and how the text is organized. The *Standardized Testing* questions relate to the content just learned.

Section 6
Extra Skill Practice

For Exercises 1–4, use the stem-and-leaf plot below.

Mark's Social Studies Test Scores

```
 7 | 7 9 9
 8 | 0 0 3 3 3 7 7 8 9
 9 | 2 4 4 6
10 | 0
```

9 | 2 → means a score of 92

1. What is Mark's lowest score?
2. What is his highest score?
3. On how many tests did Mark score an 80?
4. Find the mean, the median, and the mode of Mark's scores.

Find each quotient.

5. $0.2 \overline{)3.4}$
6. $0.05 \overline{)11.25}$
7. $1.8 \overline{)6.12}$
8. $0.3 \overline{)1.29}$
9. $0.009 \overline{)0.108}$
10. $7.5 \overline{)70.125}$
11. $1.6 \overline{)7.68}$
12. $6.12 \overline{)34.884}$
13. $0.021 \overline{)0.1953}$
14. $0.08 \overline{)5.6}$
15. $3.4 \overline{)153.68}$
16. $2.75 \overline{)8.9375}$

Standardized Testing ▶ Performance Task

Explain why the quotient is always greater than the dividend when the divisor is between 0 and 1. Include at least one example in your explanation.

$$\text{Divisor is between 0 and 1.} \overline{) \substack{\text{Quotient is greater} \\ \text{than dividend.} \\ \text{Dividend is positive.}}}$$

Module 3 Statistical Safari

Reflecting Question on the *Extra Skill Practice*

Exercises 1–4 provide extra skill practice for Exploration 1 and Exercises 5–16 for Exploration 2. The *Standardized Testing* questions help students become comfortable with various formats of standardized testing questions about the mathematical content of the section.

V. Try This as a Class How could you decide when a student should complete all or part of these exercises?

28 *Math Thematics*, Book 1

Looking at Setting the Stages

The purpose of the *Setting the Stage* is to capture students' interest and to create a context for learning the mathematics. This is done through the use of a:

- Reading—a poem, story, or article, preferably written for a middle school audience
- Activity—a game, simulation, or quiz
- Visual Display—a photo, map, chart, graph, or diagram

Examples of each type of *Setting the Stage* will be explored in this section.

The three books of *Math Thematics* contain a broad array of literature in the *Setting the Stages*, explorations, and *Practice & Application Exercises*. A complete list of literature excerpts is given below.

Fiction

Book 1:
- *The China Year* by Emily Cheney Neville
- *The Phantom Tollbooth* by Norton Juster
- *Sadako and the Thousand Paper Cranes* by Eleanor Coerr
- *Justin and the Best Biscuits in the World* by Mildred Pitts Walter
- "One Inch Tall" from *Where the Sidewalk Ends* by Shel Silverstein
- *Gulliver's Travels* by Jonathan Swift
- *The Diving Bell* by Todd Strasser
- *Skylark* by Patricia MacLachlan
- *The Day It Rained Forever* by Robert C. Lee

Book 2:
- "Smart" by Shel Silverstein from *Where the Sidewalk Ends*
- *Hatchet* by Gary Paulsen
- *Zanboomer* by R.R. Knudson
- *Banner in the Sky* by James Ramsey Ullman
- *The Horses of Central Park* by Michael Slade

Book 3:
- *American Tall Tales* by Adrien Stoutenberg
- "Paul Bunyan" from *Big Men, Big Country* by Paul Robert Walker
- *The Mystery of Blacktail Canyon*
- "The Emperor's New Clothes" by Hans Christian Anderson from *Eighty Fairy Tales*
- *Black Star, Bright Dawn* by Scott O'Dell
- "Sidewalk Measles" by Barbara M. Hales from *The Sky is Full of Song*
- *Charlie and the Chocolate Factory* by Roald Dahl
- *Black Star, Bright Dawn* by Scott O'Dell

Historical Fiction and Nonfiction

Book 1:
- *The Tracker* by Tom Brown, Jr.
- *Savage Paradise* by Hugo van Lawick
- *The Great Wall of China* by Leonard Everett Fisher
- "The Great Flood of 1993" by Barbara Brownell from *National Geographic World*
- *Mesa Verde National Park* by Ruth Shaw Radlauer
- *The Great Travelers* by Milton Rugoff

Book 2:
- "There's A Moral Here, Cougar Fans" by Jerry Kirshenbaum from *Sports Illustrated*
- "Wed., August 13, 1980" by Eloise Greenfield and Alesia Revis from *Alesia*
- *Machines* by Robert O'Brien
- *Epic of Flight: Barnstormers & Speed Kings* by Paul O'Neil and the Editors of Time-Life Books
- *City in All Directions* by Arnold Adoff

Book 3:
- "Apollo 13, Houston, We've Got a Problem." by NASA
- *Lost Moon* by Jim Lovell and Jeffrey Kluger
- *The Fractal Geometry of Nature* by Benoit Mandelbrot
- *Exploring the Titanic* by Robert D. Ballard
- *The Perfect Storm* by Sebastian Junger
- *Seeing Fingers: The Story of Louis Braille* by Etta DeGering
- *Breakthrough, Tunnelling the Channel* by Derek Wilson
- *Survivors in the Shadows* by Gary Turbak

Think About It Questions

The *Think About It* questions help deepen a student's understanding of what he or she has read, done, or seen. The questions range from simple recall to application. Often the problem to be investigated in the exploration is identified in the *Setting the Stage*.

The *Setting the Stage* and *Think About It* questions will take approximately 10 and 15 minutes to complete. There are many times when you can use the *Setting the Stage* as a launching point to other related mathematics or subject areas.

Professional Development Handbook

Using a Reading in the Setting the Stage

A reading can be a poem, a story, or an article.

EXPLORING

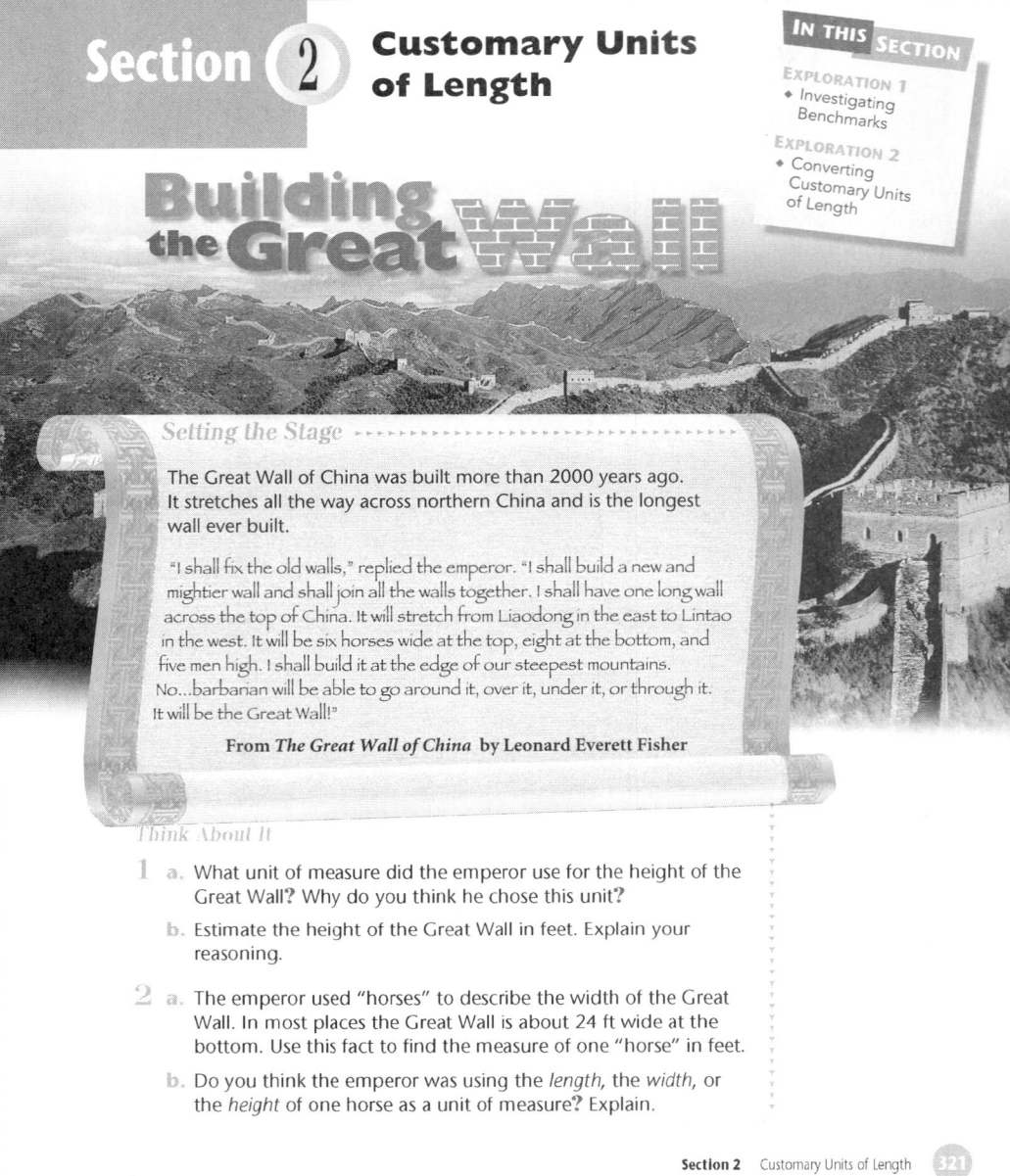

Section 2 — Customary Units of Length

IN THIS SECTION
- EXPLORATION 1
  ♦ Investigating Benchmarks
- EXPLORATION 2
  ♦ Converting Customary Units of Length

Building the Great Wall

Setting the Stage

The Great Wall of China was built more than 2000 years ago. It stretches all the way across northern China and is the longest wall ever built.

"I shall fix the old walls," replied the emperor. "I shall build a new and mightier wall and shall join all the walls together. I shall have one long wall across the top of China. It will stretch from Liaodong in the east to Lintao in the west. It will be six horses wide at the top, eight at the bottom, and five men high. I shall build it at the edge of our steepest mountains. No...barbarian will be able to go around it, over it, under it, or through it. It will be the Great Wall!"

From The Great Wall of China *by Leonard Everett Fisher*

Think About It

1. a. What unit of measure did the emperor use for the height of the Great Wall? Why do you think he chose this unit?
   b. Estimate the height of the Great Wall in feet. Explain your reasoning.

2. a. The emperor used "horses" to describe the width of the Great Wall. In most places the Great Wall is about 24 ft wide at the bottom. Use this fact to find the measure of one "horse" in feet.
   b. Do you think the emperor was using the *length*, the *width*, or the *height* of one horse as a unit of measure? Explain.

Reflecting Questions on the Reading

A. Students investigate benchmarks in Exploration 1 of this section. How do the *Setting the Stage* and *Think About It* questions help introduce the idea?

B. In Exploration 2, students discover how to convert between customary units of length. Which question in the *Think About It* has students convert units intuitively?

Section 2 Factors and Divisibility

IN THIS SECTION
EXPLORATION 1
◆ Testing for Divisibility
EXPLORATION 2
◆ Prime Factors
EXPLORATION 3
◆ Powers of Numbers

Using an Activity in the Setting the Stage

An activity can be a game, a simulation, or a quiz.

Paper Clip Products

Setting the Stage

SET UP Work with a partner. You will need: • Labsheet 2A
• 2 paper clips • 10 each of two different-colored chips

Paper Clip Products is a strategy game involving multiplication.

Paper Clip Products

- Player 1 starts. Place your two paper clips on numbers in the factor list. They may be on the same factor. Multiply the numbers and place a chip on the product on the game board. (Player 2 will use a different chip color.)

- Player 1 and Player 2 alternate turns. On a turn, leave one paper clip where it is, and move the other clip to any factor. Cover the new product with a chip.

- A turn ends when a player covers a product or if a product is not on the game board or is already covered.

- A player wins by covering three adjacent products horizontally, vertically, or diagonally.

Use Labsheet 2A. Play the *Paper Clip Products* game twice.

Think About It

1. When you were Player 1, how did you decide where to place the first two paper clips?

2. What kind of moves did you avoid? Why?

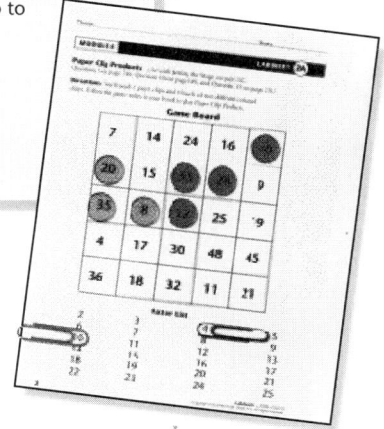

Section 2 Factors and Divisibility 247

Reflecting Questions on the Activity

C. Make a copy of the labsheet shown on the student page. Use paper clips and colored chips to play one game of *Paper Clip Products*.

D. **Discussion** What mathematical ideas could you explore with your class after playing this game? How could you get students started on them?

E. *Paper Clip Products* is a strategy game. What strategies do you think students will use?

Professional Development Handbook   31

Using a Visual Display in the Setting the Stage

A visual display can be a photo, map, chart, or diagram.

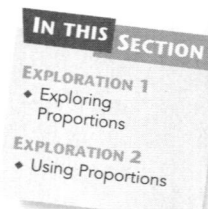

EXPLORING

Section 4 Proportions

IN THIS SECTION
- EXPLORATION 1
  • Exploring Proportions
- EXPLORATION 2
  • Using Proportions

Jumping ABILITY

Setting the Stage

Look at the table and graph to see how the world-record long jump for a human compares to the records of several animals.

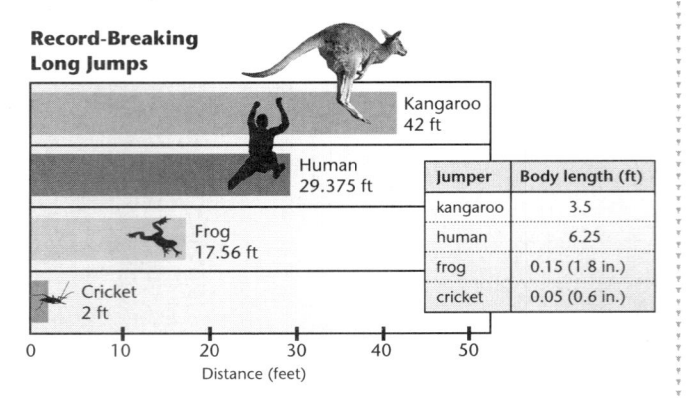

Record-Breaking Long Jumps

- Kangaroo 42 ft
- Human 29.375 ft
- Frog 17.56 ft
- Cricket 2 ft

Distance (feet): 0, 10, 20, 30, 40, 50

Jumper	Body length (ft)
kangaroo	3.5
human	6.25
frog	0.15 (1.8 in.)
cricket	0.05 (0.6 in.)

Think About It

1. **a.** Which of the four jumped the farthest?

   b. Which of the four can jump more than 10 times its body length? more than 100 times?

   c. Is it fair to compare jumping ability by examining just the distance jumped? Explain.

2. Describe how ratios written in decimal form can be used to identify which jumper traveled the farthest for its size.

Section 4 Proportions 413

Reflecting Questions on the Visual Display

F. Students have explored ratios in an earlier section. This is their first exposure to proportions in Book 1. Which question intuitively brings in the idea of proportions?

G. Based on the *Setting the Stage* and *Think About It* questions, what do you think is the "problem" students will explore in this section?

H. Try This as a Class Think about the various learning styles of students.

- Which *Setting the Stage* would most appeal to visual learners? auditory learners? kinesthetic learners?

- Would any *Setting the Stage* benefit two different types of learning styles? Explain.

Looking at Explorations

Explorations are where the mathematical concepts are developed. It is usually in the explorations that students see or make connections to other subject areas or to other mathematical concepts. Making connections is a major emphasis in *Math Thematics*. There are four unifying concepts used throughout *Math Thematics* that help students make connections and build mathematical concepts. These unifying concepts— proportional reasoning, multiple representations, patterns and generalizations, and modeling— are so powerful and so pervasive in mathematics they act as a catalyst for all mathematics at the middle school level. These four unifying concepts often overlap, so no clear delineation is drawn between them.

Proportional Reasoning

Proportional reasoning has as its central concept the representation of one quantity as a certain multiple of another. It is critical to the basic ideas of ratio, rate, "per," percent, unit ratios, proportions, slope, similarity, scale, linear functions, and probability. The language of proportions is the language of business and consumers, engineers and farmers, cooks and athletes. No topic enjoys more applications than that of proportional reasoning.

Multiple Representations

Central to the study of mathematics is the need to prepare students to interpret the world they experience in a variety of new ways and to become flexible in using mathematical tools and making connections. Multiple representations allow students to understand important mathematical ideas. A particular representation may clarify ideas more effectively for one student than another. Multiple representations include topics such as coordinate systems and functions, fraction-decimal-percent representations, spatial and numerical models of real-world situations, and geometric representations of arithmetic concepts. True understanding is often gained and enhanced by the broad use of sketches, diagrams, tables, frequency distributions, charts, graphs, physical models, computer simulations, and written and oral exposition. In addition to understanding, multiple representations allow us to ask questions that lead to greater imaging of the real world.

Patterns and Generalizations

In *Math Thematics*, students not only recognize numerical and geometric patterns, but also learn to describe them and to make, test, and utilize generalizations about the information or data gathered in a problem situation. To teach mathematics as a tool for building models of the real world, it is essential that the patterns and generalizations in mathematics be carefully articulated. Patterns and generalizations are valuable tools for developing algorithms, summarizing data, understanding recursive functions, understanding geometric concepts such as similarity and symmetry, and understanding counting techniques. Students in *Math Thematics* analyze patterns, as well as create their own.

Modeling

Mathematical modeling is a process of taking a problem from the real world, mathematizing it, finding a solution, and then interpreting and validating the solution in the real-world context. Modeling enables middle school students to understand that mathematics is connected to the real world, but that sometimes real situations are too complicated to be modeled. Examples of problems that students model in *Math Thematics* include lightning charges, the elasticity of bungee cords, and patterns in modern art.

As you read and work through the following explorations, think about how these unifying concepts are used. Do you see evidence of proportional reasoning, multiple representations, patterns and generalizations, or modeling? What other connections might you see in the *Practice & Application Exercises* or the *Module Project*?

Number Strand in Math Thematics

The number strand includes the concepts and skills associated with understanding and representing numbers, including integers. This strand also emphasizes using the place-value system and performing operations. The integer concepts are postponed until Modules 7 and 8 in Book 1 to allow students time to mature mathematically. Integer concepts and computation are introduced at an intuitive level, but move on to visual and then symbolic representations. In Books 2 and 3, students are introduced to integer ideas in the second module. The concepts are always introduced at an intuitive level, allowing students to move from one level of abstraction to another. The remaining modules in both Books 2 and 3 continue to utilize integer concepts. The chart at the right shows how the number strand spirals through all three books of *Math Thematics*.

Book 1

Module 1
- Whole Number Computation, Estimation, and Mental Math
- Order of Operations

Module 2
- Fraction, Decimal, and Mixed Number Concepts
- Add and Subtract Decimals*
- Equivalent Fractions

Module 3
- Percent Concepts
- Fraction, Decimal, and Percent Relationship
- Divide Decimals

Module 4
- Factors, Multiples, Primes, and Composites
- Exponential Form
- Multiply Fractions and Decimals*
- Mixed Number Concepts

Module 5
- Fraction and Mixed Number Concepts
- Add, Subtract, Multiply, and Divide Fractions and Mixed Numbers*

Module 6
- Ratio, Rate, and Proportion Concepts
- Estimate Percents Using Fractions

Module 7
- Comparing Integers

Module 8
- Add and Subtract Integers
- Scientific Notation
- Multiply by a Decimal to Find a Percent of a Number
- Percents Greater Than 100%

Book 2

Module 1
- Percent and Exponent Concepts Review
- Order of Operations

Module 2
- Compare Integers
- Opposite and Absolute Value
- Add and Subtract Integers
- Properties of Addition

Module 3
- Factors, Multiples, Primes and Composites
- Add and Subtract Fractions and Mixed Numbers*
- Scientific Notation

Module 4
- Multiply and Divide Fractions, Mixed Numbers, Decimals, and Integers*
- Reciprocals

Module 5
- Ratio, Rate, and Proportion Concepts
- Find Percents
- Fraction, Decimal, and Percent Relationship

Module 6
- Inequalities
- Approximate and Find Square Roots
- Write Proportions in Context

Module 7
- Percent Greater than 100%*
- Percents less than 1%
- Percent of Change

Book 3

Module 1
- Rate, Ratio, and Exponent Review*

Module 2
- Solve Proportions
- Find Percents and Percent of Change
- Add, Subtract, Multiply, and Divide Integers

Module 3
- Approximate and Find Square Roots
- Order of Operations
- Scientific Notation

Module 4
- Multiply and Divide Rational Numbers

Module 5
- Zero and Negative Exponents
- Scientific Notation
- Properties of Exponents

Module 6
- Ratio Applications
- Inequalities

* includes mental math and estimation

Exploration

Adding
+ Integers

GOAL

LEARN HOW TO...
- add integers

AS YOU...
- play the game *Thunderbolt!*

KEY TERM
- opposites

SET UP Work with a partner. You will need: • Labsheet 1A
• 12 beans, each marked with a "+" on one side and a "–" on the other side • paper cup • 2 game pieces

▶ Like other sparks of static electricity, lightning gets its power from the difference in the electrical charges of two objects. You will simulate the changing charges in a cloud by playing the game *Thunderbolt!* When the difference in charges is 10 or more—Zap!

3 **Use Labsheet 1A.** Follow the directions on the labsheet to play *Thunderbolt!* Play the game two times.

4 **a.** Did you find a way to quickly determine where to place your game piece after a bean toss? Explain.

   b. At the end of a turn, can your game piece ever be an even number of units away from where it was at the start of your turn? Why?

   c. At the end of a turn, can your game piece ever be in the same place it was when you started the turn? Why?

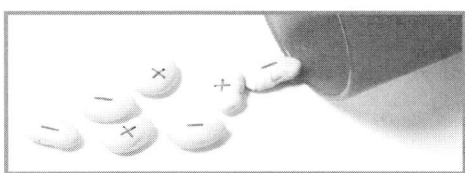

5 **a.** If you played *Thunderbolt!* with only six beans, what moves would be possible?

   b. Would playing with only six beans change your answers to Questions 4(b) and 4(c)? Explain.

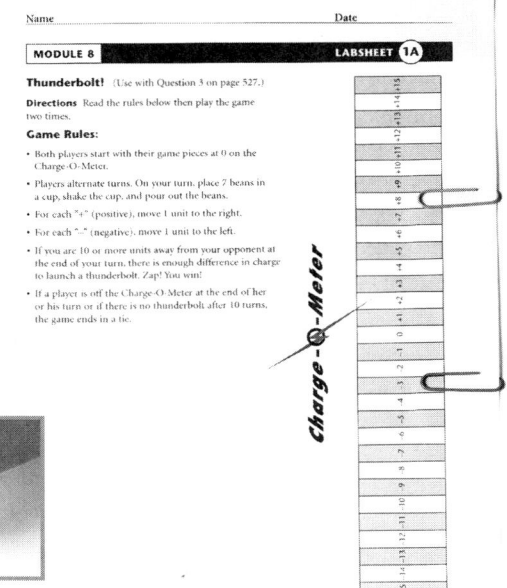

Section 1 Adding and Subtracting Integers

Professional Development Handbook **35**

Name _____ Date _____

MODULE 8 **LABSHEET 1A**

Thunderbolt! (Use with Question 3 on page 527.)

Directions Read the rules below. Then play the game two times.

Game Rules:

- Both players start with their game pieces at 0 on the Charge-O-Meter.

- Players alternate turns. On your turn, place 7 beans in a cup, shake the cup, and pour out the beans.

- For each "+" (positive), move 1 unit to the right.

- For each "−" (negative), move 1 unit to the left.

- If you are 10 or more units away from your opponent at the end of your turn, there is enough difference in charge to launch a thunderbolt. Zap! You win!

- If a player is off the Charge-O-Meter at the end of her or his turn or if there is no thunderbolt after 10 turns, the game ends in a tie.

Charge-O-Meter: −15, −14, −13, −12, −11, −10, −9, −8, −7, −6, −5, −4, −3, −2, −1, 0, +1, +2, +3, +4, +5, +6, +7, +8, +9, +10, +11, +12, +13, +14, +15

▶ One strategy for quickly finding how far to move your game piece is to pair positive beans with negative beans. This strategy can also be used to model addition of integers.

EXAMPLE

Suppose you tossed 5 positive beans and 2 negative beans.

2 positive beans can be paired with 2 negative beans to cancel each other out.

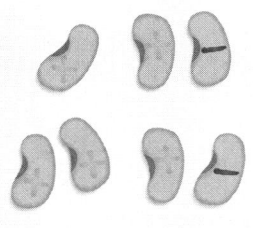

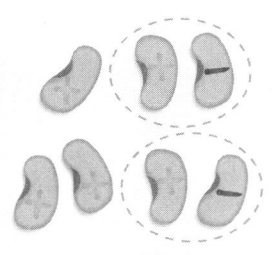

+5 + –2 = ?

6 Discussion Look at the addition in the Example.

a. Why do the paired beans cancel each other out?

b. If you tossed the combination of beans shown, how far would you move your game piece and in what direction?

c. What integer is represented by the combination of beans?

d. +5 + (–2) = ?

To avoid confusion a negative integer can be shown in parentheses.

✓ **QUESTION 7**

...checks that you can represent integer addition using a bean model.

7 ✓ CHECKPOINT

a. Suppose you had 24 beans in your cup and you tossed 14 negative beans and 10 positive beans. How would you move your game piece?

b. Write an integer addition equation for the combination of beans in part (a).

8 Use a bean model to find each sum.

a. +1 + (–5)   b. +6 + (–4)   c. +3 + (–3)   d. –5 + (–2)

Module 8 Our Environment

Use beans to help answer Questions 9–11.

9 **Try This As a Class**

   a. Write two different addition equations where both addends (the numbers that are added) are negative.

   b. Is the sum of two negative numbers positive or negative?

   c. How can you find the sum of two negative numbers without using beans?

10 Write two different examples for each case.

Case	Examples
a. one addend is positive, one addend is negative, the sum is a positive integer	
b. one addend is positive, one addend is negative, the sum is a negative integer	
c. one addend is positive, one addend is negative, the sum is zero	

11 **Discussion** When will the sum of a positive and a negative integer be positive? negative? equal to 0?

12 How can you find the sum of a positive and a negative integer without using beans?

13 **Try This as a Class** The numbers you used to answer Question 10(c) are *opposites*. What do think it means for two numbers to be **opposites**?

▶ It is not necessary to label positive integers with a "+" sign. For example, +3 is the same as 3.

14 ✓ **CHECKPOINT** Find each sum without using beans.

   a. –17 + 25   b. 13 + (–7)   c. –36 + (–9)
   d. –11 + 11   e. –24 + 19   f. 12 + (–17)

✓ **QUESTION 14**
...checks that you can add integers.

HOMEWORK EXERCISES ▶ See Exs. 1–21 on pp. 534–535.

Section 1 Adding and Subtracting Integers

Reflecting Questions on Exploration 1

Use student pages 527–529 and Labsheet 1A (pp. 35–38 of this handbook).

A. Complete Questions 3–6 with a partner.

B. What integer concepts are intuitively explored in Questions 4 and 5?

C. **Try This as a Class** Look at the Example on page 528. How does the Example help students make the connection between the concrete model and the symbolic representation of $5 + (-2)$?

Checkpoints are used to quickly assess whether a student understands a newly explored concept. They are usually at a basic skill level but can sometimes be an application or extension of what was just learned.

D. **Discussion** Look at the two *Checkpoints* in this exploration (Questions 7 and 14). What type of questioning is used in each?

Try This as a Class questions are used for a variety of reasons. This type of question might be a teacher demonstration, class discussion, guided discovery, or summarization of the content.

E. What role does the teacher play in Question 9? Question 13?

F. Which questions in this exploration encourage students to determine their own integer algorithms?

G. **Discussion** Suppose a student answers Question 12, "I would subtract the smaller number from the bigger number, and my answer would have the sign of the bigger number." What would you, as the teacher, say to this student?

Probability Strand in Math Thematics

EXPLORING

An understanding of probability and the related area of statistics is essential to being an informed citizen. Often we read statements such as, "There is a 20 percent chance of rain or snow today." "The odds are three to two that the Cats will win the championship." "The probability of winning the grand prize in the state lottery is 1 in 7,240,000." Students in the middle grades have an intense interest in the notions of fairness and the chances of winning games. The study of probability develops concepts and methods for investigating such situations. These methods allow students to make predictions when uncertainty exists and to make sense of claims that they see and hear.

—NCTM *Curriculum and Evaluation Standards for School Mathematics,* 1989

In *Math Thematics*, students experience probability in a broad range of contexts. Some of the areas students explore include games of strategy, meteor showers, basketball, parachuting, store contests, searching for the *Titanic,* and locks and keys. Students make predictions and explain events by collecting data and using mathematical models. In all three books of *Math Thematics*, students determine the theoretical and experimental probabilities of events and make predictions based on experimental results. Students also learn how to devise, carry out, and interpret simulations involving probability. The repetition of some concepts and the introduction of new concepts allow students to deepen their understanding of probability and make connections to other subject areas. This spiraling of the probability concepts is shown in the chart below.

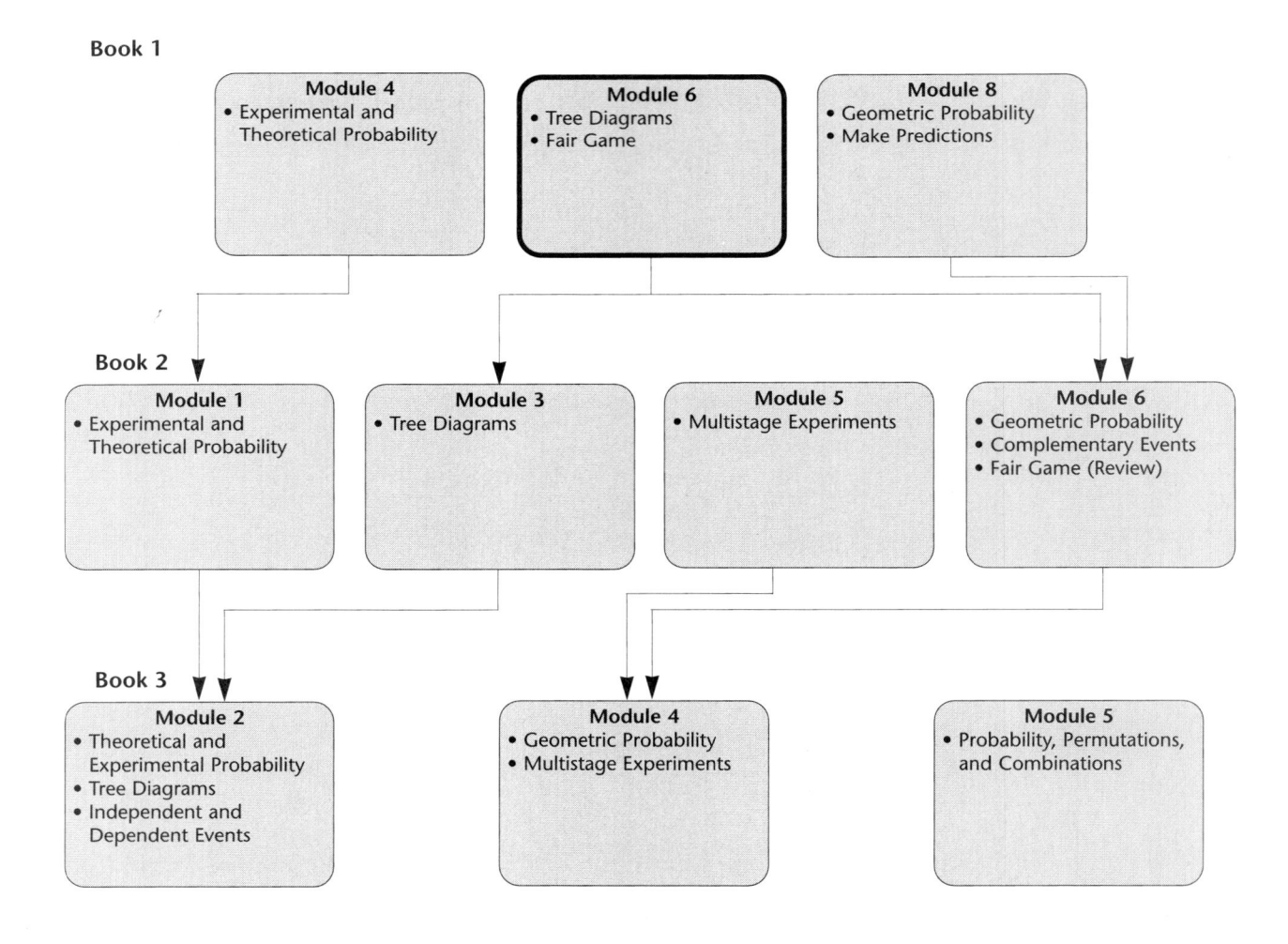

Book 1

Module 4
- Experimental and Theoretical Probability

Module 6
- Tree Diagrams
- Fair Game

Module 8
- Geometric Probability
- Make Predictions

Book 2

Module 1
- Experimental and Theoretical Probability

Module 3
- Tree Diagrams

Module 5
- Multistage Experiments

Module 6
- Geometric Probability
- Complementary Events
- Fair Game (Review)

Book 3

Module 2
- Theoretical and Experimental Probability
- Tree Diagrams
- Independent and Dependent Events

Module 4
- Geometric Probability
- Multistage Experiments

Module 5
- Probability, Permutations, and Combinations

Exploration 2

TR‹EE DIAGRAMS

GOAL

LEARN HOW TO...
- make a tree diagram to find probabilities

AS YOU...
- play the game *Dueling Spinners*

KEY TERMS
- fair game
- tree diagram

SET UP Work with a partner. You will need: • Labsheets 6B and 6C • paper clip

▶ Softball is based on skill, but there are many games that rely on a lucky roll of a die or flip of a coin. You'll predict the results of the game *Dueling Spinners* and then examine the probability of winning to see if the game is fair.

Game Rules You and your partner each spin a spinner. Whoever spins the greater number is the winner.

Use Labsheet 6B for Questions 13–16.

13 Decide who will use Spinner A and who will use Spinner B. Do you think Spinner A or Spinner B will win more often? Explain your reasoning.

14 a. Play *Dueling Spinners* ten times. Record the winning spinner for each game on the labsheet.

b. How do your results in part (a) compare with your prediction in Question 13?

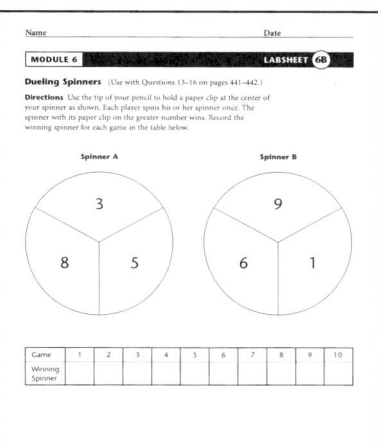

Section 6 Percents and Probability

Name _____ Date _____

MODULE 6 **LABSHEET 6B**

Dueling Spinners (Use with Questions 13–16 on pages 441–442.)

Directions Use the tip of your pencil to hold a paper clip at the center of your spinner. Each player spins his or her spinner once. The spinner with its paper clip on the greater number wins. Record the winning spinner for each game in the table below.

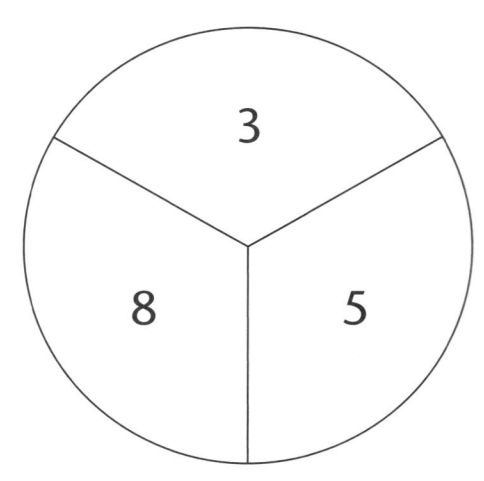

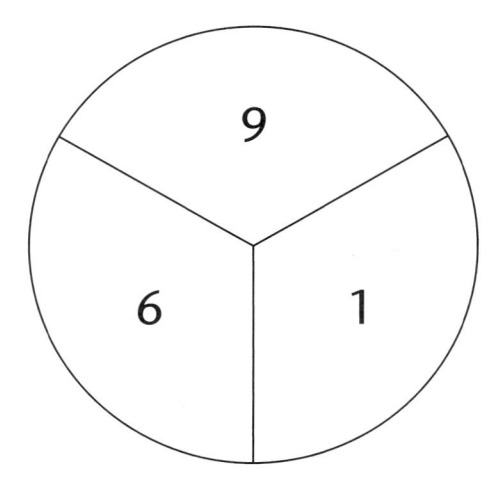

Spinner A: 3, 8, 5

Spinner B: 9, 6, 1

Game	1	2	3	4	5	6	7	8	9	10
Winning Spinner										

Copyright © by McDougal Littell Inc. All rights reserved.

Math Thematics, Book 1 **6-55**

Math Thematics, Book 1

15 Try This as a Class Combine your results with the results of the rest of the class.

a. How many times did Spinner A win?

b. How many times did Spinner B win?

c. How do the class results compare with your individual results and your prediction in Question 13?

▶ In a **fair game** each player has an equal chance of winning. Playing a game can help you decide if it is fair, but you may need to play many times to be sure. Another way to decide if a game is fair is to list and compare all the possible outcomes.

16 Discussion Look at the spinners on Labsheet 6B.

a. What are the possible outcomes when Spinner A is spun?

b. Are the outcomes equally likely? Explain.

c. Suppose the outcome on Spinner A is 3. What are the possible outcomes for Spinner B? Are the outcomes for Spinner B equally likely?

d. Would your answers to part (c) be the same if the outcome on Spinner A was 5 or 8? Explain.

> FOR ◀ HELP
> with *equally likely outcomes*, see
> **MODULE 4, p. 242**

▶ A **tree diagram** can be used to find and organize the possible outcomes for a game. The steps below show how to make a tree diagram for *Dueling Spinners*.

First
Draw branches for the outcomes of Spinner A.

Spinner A

③
⑤
⑧

Then
Add branches for the outcomes of Spinner B.

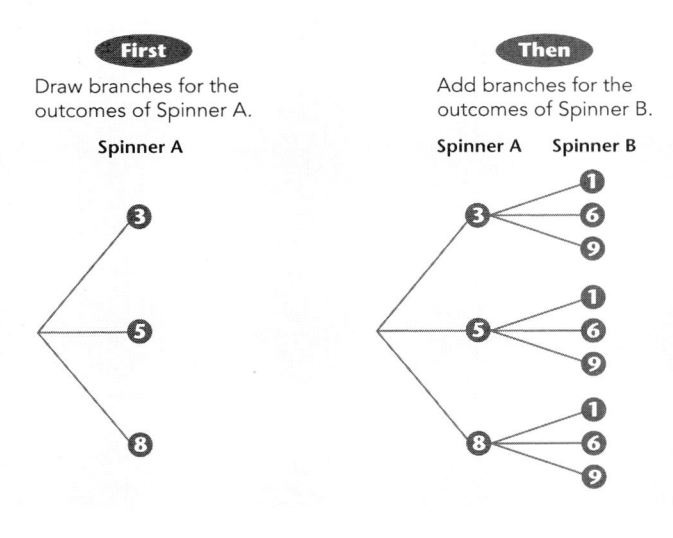

Spinner A   Spinner B

③ — ①, ⑥, ⑨
⑤ — ①, ⑥, ⑨
⑧ — ①, ⑥, ⑨

442   Module 6   Comparisons and Predictions

17 **Use Labsheet 6C.** Follow the directions for the *Tree Diagram*. You'll find the number of times each spinner wins and then compare probabilities to decide if the game is fair.

▶ Suppose you are going to play the *Dueling Spinners* game using Spinner C below. Your opponent will use either Spinner D or Spinner E.

Spinner C   Spinner D   Spinner E

18 **Try This as a Class**

  a. Make a tree diagram to show the outcomes for Spinner C versus Spinner D.

  b. Find the probability that Spinner C will beat Spinner D.

19 ✓ **CHECKPOINT** Use a tree diagram to find the probability that Spinner C will beat Spinner E.

✓ **QUESTION 19**

...checks that you can make a tree diagram and use it to find probabilities.

▶ **Using Percent Form** Probabilities can be written and then compared as percents.

20 Use your answers from Questions 18 and 19.

  a. What percent of the time would you expect Spinner C to beat Spinner D?

  b. What percent of the time would you expect Spinner C to beat Spinner E?

  c. Which spinner does Spinner C have a better chance of beating, D or E?

21 **Discussion** When you answered Question 20(c), was it easier to use the percent form of the probabilities or the fraction form that you found in Questions 18 and 19? Explain.

HOMEWORK EXERCISES ▶ See Exs. 20–28 on pp. 446–447.

Name _____ Date _____

MODULE 6   **LABSHEET 6C**

Tree Diagram (Use with Question 17 on page 443.)

Directions Use the tree diagram below to complete parts (a)–(g).

a. Trace along the branches of the tree diagram and list the possible outcomes. One entry has been done for you.

b. For each outcome, decide which spinner wins and list the letter beside the outcome.

c. Count the winning outcomes for Spinner A.

d. Write a ratio in fraction form that compares the total number of winning outcomes for Spinner A to the total number of outcomes. This is the probability that Spinner A wins.

e. Find the probability that Spinner B wins.

f. How is the probability that Spinner A wins related to the probability that Spinner B wins?

g. Is *Dueling Spinners* a fair game? Explain.

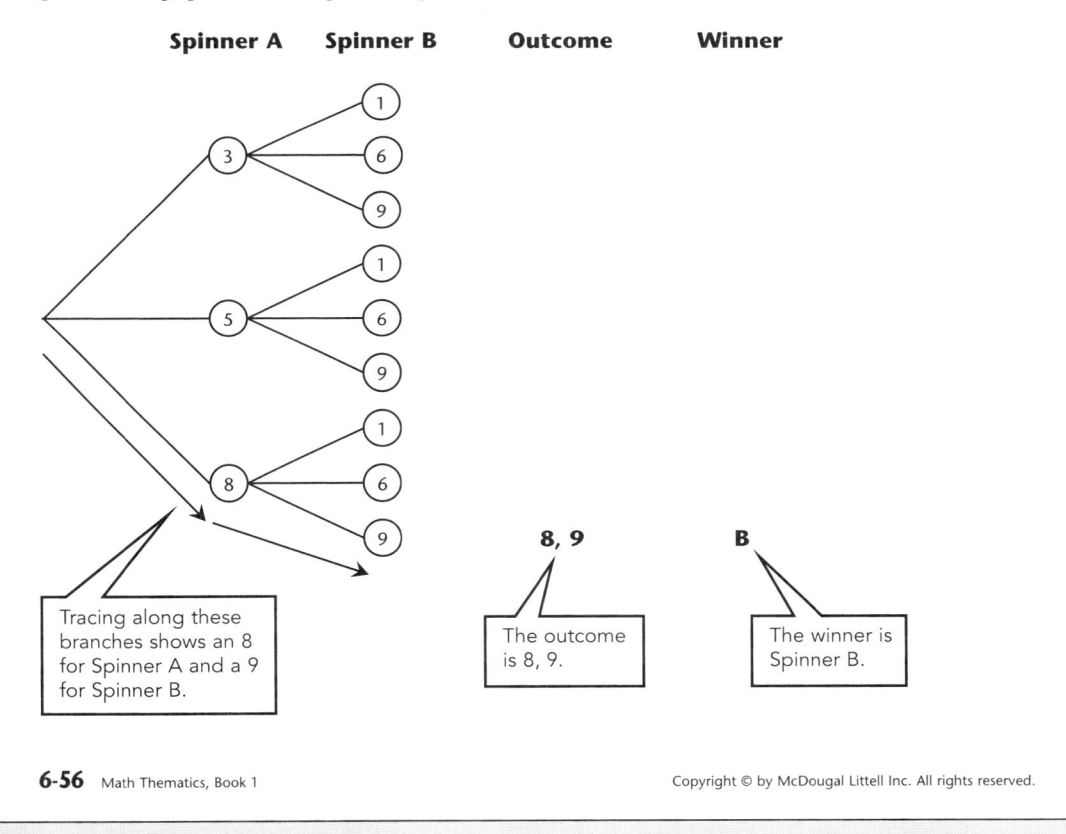

Spinner A   Spinner B   Outcome   Winner

3 → 1, 6, 9
5 → 1, 6, 9
8 → 1, 6, 9

8, 9   B

Tracing along these branches shows an 8 for Spinner A and a 9 for Spinner B.

The outcome is 8, 9.

The winner is Spinner B.

Reflecting Questions on Exploration 2

Use student pages 441–443 and Labsheets 6B and 6C (pp. 41–45 of this handbook).

H. Read the introductory paragraph and complete Questions 13 and 14 with a partner.

I. What "problem" are students trying to solve in this exploration?

J. Complete Questions 16 and 17. What models are used to help students solve the "problem"?

K. **Discussion** Look back at your answer to Question 13 in the exploration.

- Did you correctly guess which spinner should win more often? What would you expect students to answer?

- How does Question 13 help stimulate students' interest?

L. Before starting this exploration, students should be familiar with the idea of probability, but mastery of probability is not expected. What features or questions provide help with probability ideas?

M. It is important for students to compare theoretical and experimental probabilities and discuss the reasons for the differences between the two.

- Use your results from Question 14 to determine the experimental probability that your spinner would win.

- How did the theoretical probability you found in Question 17 compare to the experimental probability? Why might they not be the same?

N. **Journal** Was it important for you, as a teacher, to work through many of the questions in this exploration? Why or why not?

Looking at Technology

Calculators and computers are tools that help make sense of mathematical concepts by allowing students to display results, to find patterns, and to ask and answer "What if ... ?" questions. To achieve mathematical power, students must learn to select appropriate tools and techniques and to use them effectively.

Technology is used throughout the *Math Thematics* curriculum to develop and reinforce mathematical ideas and concepts, solve problems, and bridge the gap between the classroom and real-world activities. The materials, however, are designed so that they do not depend on the use of technology.

Calculators

The *Math Thematics* curriculum assumes that every student will have access to a scientific calculator in class. For Book 3, a scientific calculator is needed for homework as well. There are also optional questions for use with a calculator with fraction capability in Books 1–3 and for a graphing calculator in Books 2 and 3. Besides being used for computation, calculators are used throughout the materials to generate data, to reinforce concepts, and to develop new content and procedures. The following is an example from Section 3 of Module 2 in Book 1.

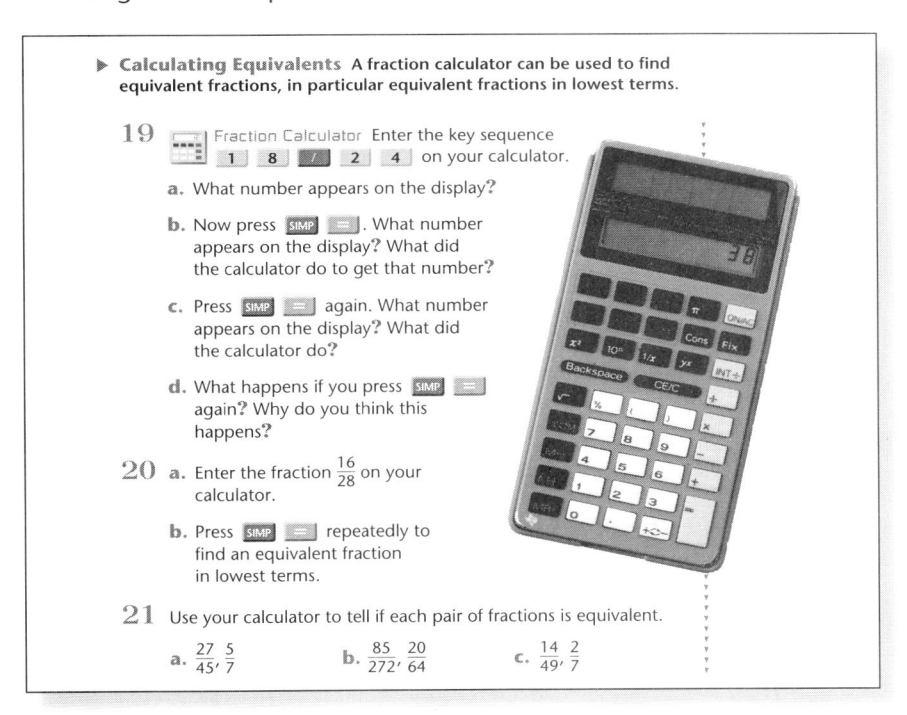

▶ **Calculating Equivalents** A fraction calculator can be used to find equivalent fractions, in particular equivalent fractions in lowest terms.

19 Fraction Calculator Enter the key sequence `1` `8` `/` `2` `4` on your calculator.

   a. What number appears on the display?

   b. Now press `SIMP` `=`. What number appears on the display? What did the calculator do to get that number?

   c. Press `SIMP` `=` again. What number appears on the display? What did the calculator do?

   d. What happens if you press `SIMP` `=` again? Why do you think this happens?

20 a. Enter the fraction $\frac{16}{28}$ on your calculator.

    b. Press `SIMP` `=` repeatedly to find an equivalent fraction in lowest terms.

21 Use your calculator to tell if each pair of fractions is equivalent.

   a. $\frac{27}{45}, \frac{5}{7}$ b. $\frac{85}{272}, \frac{20}{64}$ c. $\frac{14}{49}, \frac{2}{7}$

Reflecting Questions on Using Calculators

A. Answer Question 19.

B. How does the use of a fraction calculator in Question 19 help to develop ideas about equivalent fractions and expressing fractions in lowest terms?

Professional Development Handbook

Other Technology

Most modules contain a resource page that introduces a type of technology like graphing calculators, spreadsheets, drawing software, graphing utilities, or probability and statistics packages. These pages explain how to use appropriate technology as an alternative method for completing an exploration. The following example is from Section 4 of Module 2 in Book 1.

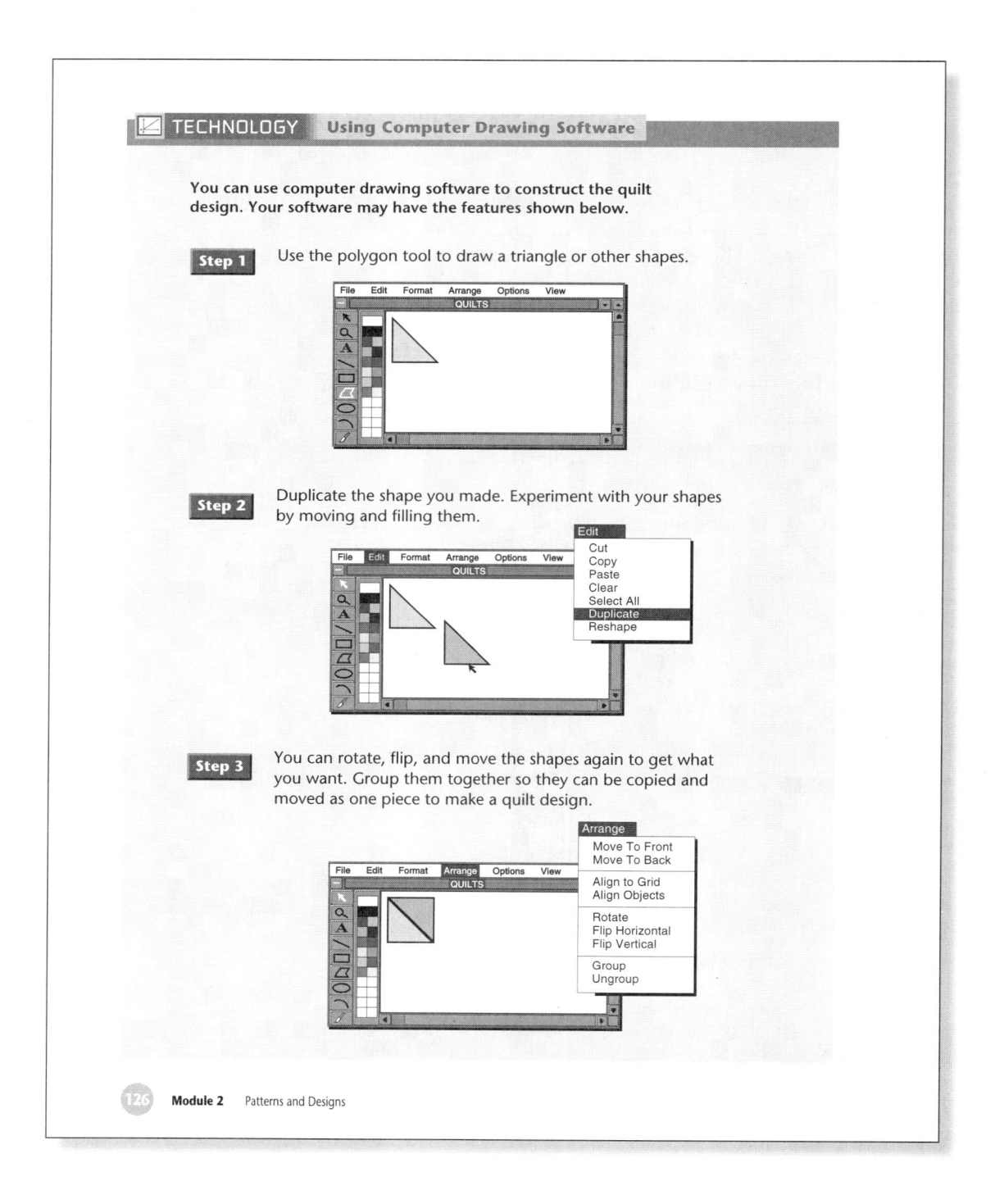

TECHNOLOGY — Using Computer Drawing Software

You can use computer drawing software to construct the quilt design. Your software may have the features shown below.

Step 1 Use the polygon tool to draw a triangle or other shapes.

Step 2 Duplicate the shape you made. Experiment with your shapes by moving and filling them.

Edit menu:
- Cut
- Copy
- Paste
- Clear
- Select All
- Duplicate
- Reshape

Step 3 You can rotate, flip, and move the shapes again to get what you want. Group them together so they can be copied and moved as one piece to make a quilt design.

Arrange menu:
- Move To Front
- Move To Back
- Align to Grid
- Align Objects
- Rotate
- Flip Horizontal
- Flip Vertical
- Group
- Ungroup

126 Module 2 Patterns and Designs

The Authors' Answers to Reflecting Questions

This section contains answers to the questions in the *Exploring Math Thematics* section.

Close-Up of a Section

Reflecting Questions on the Setting the Stage (p. 11)

A. *This module contains six sections, but this is the only one about dinosaurs. What other animals do you think students would find interesting? Is there one animal topic that would appeal to all students? Explain.*

Because middle school students are so diverse in their interests and maturity levels, we have tried to appeal to as many students as possible. We know that not every student will be interested in dinosaurs, so we included sections that focus on other animals—lions, gazelles, dogs, cats, fish, and many more.

B. *What is a follow-up question you could ask students after Question 2 in the* Think About It?

After students have estimated the number of days, you could discuss the estimation strategies they used or what might be true of a 4-ton *Tyrannosaurus rex*.

Reflecting Questions on Exploration 1 (p. 16)

C. *Look at the* Goal, Key Term, *and* Set Up *on page 219. Which should students read? Which can help you, as the teacher, with classroom management?*

We do not expect students to read the *Goal* statement. This is included to give teachers a brief summary of the exploration. Students should be made aware of the *Key Terms*, since it lists important vocabulary and can serve as an advanced organizer for students who may need it. Both students and teachers should read the *Set Up* to be sure they have the materials for the activity. The *Set Up* also lists the most appropriate class set up—whole class, small groups, or individual.

E. *Archeologists have categorized dinosaur lengths as small, medium, and large. Based on the stem-and-leaf plot on page 219, what size best describes the* Euoplocephalus? *Why? Based on your stem-and-leaf plot for Question 7 on page 220, what size best describes the* Tyrannosaurus rex? *Why?*

Euoplocephalus: medium; If you use catagories based on the clusters and gaps in the plot, the 7 ft dinosaur is small and those 16 ft through 25 ft are medium.

T rex: large or very large; It's the longest predator given. *The Illustrated Dinosaur Dictionary* by Helen Roney Sattler states:

[Scientists] *call theropods [the meat–eaters] that are 0 to 5 feet long very small. Those 5 to 10 feet are called small; 10 to 23 feet are medium; 23 to 35 feet are large; 35 to 50 feet long are very large; and over 50 feet long are extremely large.*

F. *What process do students go through to learn how to make a stem-and-leaf plot? How is the teacher involved in this process?*

Rather than telling students immediately how to construct a stem-and-leaf plot, we include exercises like Questions 3 and 4 to explore the plot. Teachers lead students through the process of figuring out how to interpret the stem-and-leaf plot. In Question 5 (Labsheet 6A), teachers help students construct a stem-and-leaf plot step by step. Students also spend time comparing the two plots. Although students discover some of the aspects of constructing these plots, direct instruction is usually needed.

G. *Why do you think the class was brought together for Question 5? Are there other situations in which you would bring your class together to answer a question? Explain.*

The class is brought together in Question 5 (Labsheet 6A) so that the teacher can demonstrate the process of constructing a stem-and-leaf plot. The class can be brought together to develop an algorithm, bring closure to an idea, pool data, watch a demonstration, or complete a more challenging problem.

Reflecting Questions on Exploration 2 (p. 21)

H. *What "problem" are students trying to solve?*

Students are trying to determine how many animals a *Microvenator* needed to catch and eat each day to survive. Most explorations are driven by the need to answer a question or solve a problem. The "problem" answers the question, "Why do we have to learn this?"

I. *Students use a model in Questions 9 and 10 to divide by a decimal. Is a model used for the rest of the exploration? If not, what learning technique is used?*

Students use patterns in the later questions to develop the concept of dividing by a decimal.

J. *How does Question 9 help students conceptualize division with decimals?*

A 10 × 10 grid is used to model the division. Since no one model, algorithm, or activity will work for every student, it is important to include a variety of teaching techniques. The 10 × 10 grid model works well with visual and kinesthetic learners.

L. *What does Question 10 assess? Question 14? What would you do if students understood and could answer Question 10 correctly but had difficulty with Question 14?*

Both questions assess whether students can divide by a decimal, but in Question 10, students use a model. By Question 14, students should be able to divide any number by a decimal.

If students can use the model to divide, then they are beginning to understand the concept. Questions 11–13 use patterns to develop the concept of decimal division. By examining a student's work, the teacher should be able to tell if the student is having trouble with the position of the decimal, the idea of equivalent expressions, or basic math facts.

M. *Discussion questions can be explored in pairs, groups of four, or as a class. Look at the two Discussion questions in Exploration 2 (Questions 11 and 13). What group size would you use to talk about each of them? What factors would influence your decision?*

Because the pattern identified in Question 11 is critical to the concept development, it may be best to discuss this question as a class. Question 13 can be discussed in pairs with a brief class discussion to summarize the groups' finding. The academic and maturity levels of students should be a factor in deciding how *Discussion* questions will be managed.

Discussion questions are one place where students communicate about mathematics. At what other points in an exploration do students communicate about mathematics? Is the communication always in an oral format? Explain.

Communicating about and through mathematics, both orally and in writing, is embedded in the *Math Thematics* curriculum. The teacher should identify which questions can be answered orally rather than in writing before beginning an exploration. If students have had little experience writing in math class, the teacher may need to phase in more writing activities over a period of months, combining both oral and writing activities at first.

Reflecting Questions on the *Key Concepts* (p. 22)

N. *How does Question 16 help reinforce the ideas presented in the exploration? How does this question help students understand why you might want to use a stem-and-leaf plot?*

Students need to be able to read a stem-and-leaf plot to answer Question 16. Since the data in a stem-and-leaf plot are organized from the least to the greatest value, it is relatively easy to find the median, mode, and range.

O. *Students never formally describe a rule for dividing by a decimal. How does Question 17 help students further clarify the steps for dividing by a decimal?*

The steps for dividing by a decimal are given on the *Key Concepts* page, but in Question 17, students are asked to explain how they know the division is complete. Explaining makes students reflect on the steps and why the procedure works.

Reflecting Questions on the *Practice & Application Exercises* (p. 27)

P. *Where in the section are the homework exercises identified? Which exercises repeat some of the development in the exploration? Which exercises extend the ideas in the exploration?*

The *Practice & Application Exercises* that could be assigned as homework are identified at the end of each exploration (see student page 220). The *Teacher's Resource Book* also includes an assignment guide for regular and block scheduling.

Exercises 1–5 review the development in Exploration 1 on reading stem-and-leaf plots. Exercises 6 and 7 have students practice creating stem-and-leaf plots. Exercise 8 extends students' thinking by looking at how the data are clustered in a stem-and-leaf plot. Exercises 9–12 have students examine two displays of the same data. This is the start of the process of choosing an appropriate representation. Students will come back to this idea many times in *Math Thematics*.

Q. *Exercises 13, 17, 19, 23, and 24 are embedded assessment items for dividing by a decimal. Why do you think these exercises were chosen?*

The exercises assess whether students can divide a whole number by a decimal and divide a decimal by a decimal.

R. *Why do you think Exercise 25 is a Challenge problem?*

Students must interpret the quotient and remainder in a real-world context. Students may also consider the waste caused by the cut.

S. *How does the Reflecting on the Section question (Exercise 26) help students see the connection between the statistics and number strands? What other ideas do students explore in this exercise?*

Students work backward from the stem-and-leaf plots to get raw data to find the mean. To calculate the mean, students divide with a decimal.

T. *Read over the Extension on page 227. Why might students have trouble reading a back-to-back stem-and-leaf plot?*

Back-to-back stem-and-leaf plots can be difficult to read because the left side is read backward.

U. *What math concepts are needed to complete Exercises 42 and 43?*

Students need to be able to divide and add with decimals.

Reflecting Questions on the Extra Skill Practice (p. 28)

V. *How could you decide when a student should complete all or part of these exercises?*

Students who have trouble with the homework, especially the embedded assessment items, should be assigned the appropriate exercises from Exercises 1–16. The *Standardized Testing* should be assigned to all students.

Looking at Setting the Stages

Reflecting Questions on the Reading (p. 30)

A. *Students investigate benchmarks in Exploration 1 of this section. How do the Setting the Stage and Think About It questions help introduce the idea?*

The emperor used benchmarks of the width of a horse and height of a man, and students are asked to interpret these measures in terms of a standard unit.

B. *In Exploration 2, students discover how to convert between customary units of length. Which question in the Think About It has students convert units intuitively?*

Students convert from men's heights to feet in Question 1(b), and from feet to horses' widths in Question 2(a).

Reflecting Questions on the Activity (p. 31)

D. *What mathematical ideas could you explore with your class after playing this game? How could you get students started on them?*

By asking students questions about their strategy, the game board set up, or the factor list, the teacher could introduce ideas such as, divisibility rules, factors, prime factorization, or powers.

E. *Paper Clip Products is a strategy game. What strategies do you think students will use?*

Students may block their opponent by covering a product, try to get a 2 × 2 square of numbers, or avoid products that are near prime numbers.

Reflecting Questions on the Visual Display (p. 32)

F. *Students have explored ratios in an earlier section. This is their first exposure to proportions in Book 1. Which question intuitively brings in the idea of proportion?*

Question 1(b) uses proportional reasoning with familiar wording ("10 times").

G. *Based on the Setting the Stage and Think About It questions, what do you think is the "problem" students will explore in this section?*

Students explore the relationship between the jump length and body length of each jumper.

H. *Which Setting the Stage would most appeal to visual learners? auditory learners? kinesthetic learners? Would any Setting the Stage benefit two different types of learning styles? Explain.*

The *Great Walll of China* reading appeals to visual learners, and if read aloud, to auditory learners. *Paper Clip Products* appeals to kinesthetic learners. The *Record Breaking Long Jumps* chart appeals to visual learners.

Looking at Explorations

Reflecting Questions on Exploration 1 (p. 39)

B. *What integer concepts are intuitively explored in Questions 4 and 5?*

Students intuitively explore integer addition and subtraction and opposites in Questions 4 and 5.

C. *Look at the Example on page 528. How does the Example help students make the connection between the concrete model and the symbolic representation of 5 + (−2)?*

Students begin Exploration 1 by playing *Thunderbolt!* This game intuitively explores addition and subtraction of integers. Students move to the left for each negative bean and to the right for each positive bean. After a few turns, students will notice that they can pair one negative bean with one positive bean to get a move of zero. The Example shows a picture of a possible bean toss and the pairing of a positive bean and a negative bean. The equation that describes the toss is also given. Students can use their experiences with the game to make sense of the expression 5 + (−2).

D. *Look at the two Checkpoints in this exploration (Questions 7 and 14). What type of questioning is used in each?*

The *Checkpoint* at Question 7 has students make a connection between the concrete model used in the game and the symbolic representation for the move. The *Checkpoint* at Question 14 is at a basic skill level, and assumes students understand the concept well enough to evaluate the expressions without using the bean model or pictures.

E. *What role does the teacher play in Question 9? Question 13?*

In Question 9, the teacher helps students refine their understanding of integer addition. As a class, and with the teacher's guidance, students can develop a set of examples and "rules" for integer addition. This is a critical step toward understanding the concept. In Question 13, the teacher elicits class discussion to define opposite.

F. *Which questions in this exploration encourage students to determine their own integer algorithms?*

Questions 9–12 allow students to discover the "rules" for adding integers. The understanding builds with each question. Thus, the discussion that takes place in Question 9 is critical to students succeeding in Question 10. Likewise, the discussion in Question 11 reinforces the examples students wrote in Question 10. By Question 12, students should be able to state their own rule for integer addition.

G. *Suppose a students answers Question 12, "I would subtract the smaller number from the bigger number, and my answer would have the sign of the bigger number." What would you, as the teacher, say to the student?*

We would say, "Terrific! You're getting it!" We do not expect students to use vocabulary such as *opposite*, *absolute value*, or *addend* at this point and throughout Book 1.

Reflecting Questions on Exploration 2 (p. 46)

I. *What "problem" are students trying to solve in this exploration?*

Students are trying to determine if the game is fair.

J. *What models are used to help students solve the "problem"?*

Students first use a physical model (spinners) to get an intuitive idea if the spinner game is fair. By playing the game, they develop some sense of "fairness." The spinners are then informally analyzed for various outcomes. In Question 17 (Labsheet 6C), students use a tree diagram to formally analyze the outcomes of the spinners.

K. *How does Question 13 help stimulate student interest?*

By stating in Question 13 which spinner is most likely to win, students have made a stake in the exploration. They want to know if their guess is correct and some students may want to know how you can tell which spinner is best.

L. *Before starting this exploration, students should be familiar with the idea of probability, but mastery of probability is not expected. What features or questions provide help with probability ideas?*

The *For Help* box on page 442 refers students back to Module 4 if they need to review the meaning of *equally likely outcomes*. Labsheet 6C gives the definition of *probability* in part (d) of the directions.

M. *How did the theoretical probability you found in Question 17 compare to the experimental probability? Why might they not be the same?*

Experimental probabilities, no matter how ideal the conditions, rarely have the exact same value as theoretical probabilities. The experimental probability should become relatively close to the theoretical probability as the number of trials increase. In this experiment, the bends in the paper clips, the way the spinner is spun, and the table surface can all contribute to less than ideal conditions.

N. *Was it important for you, as a teacher, to work through many of the questions in this exploration? Why or why not?*

Because of the interactive nature of this curriculum, it is important for the teacher to be aware of the possible questions their students might ask and of the problems they might encounter. Using this curriculum often means learning alongside your students.

Looking at Technology

Reflecting Questions on Using Calculators (p. 47)

B. *How does the use of a fraction calculator in Question 19 help to develop ideas about equivalent fractions and expressing fractions in lowest terms?*

In Exploration 2 of this section, students learned to express a fraction in lowest terms by dividing both the numerator and the denominator by their greatest common divisor. By explaining what operations the calculator does as it simplifies a fraction, they learn that they do not have to begin with the greatest common divisor to simplify a fraction. They also learn that one efficient technique for simplifying is to divide the numerator and the denominator by their common prime factors.

ASSESSMENT in Math Thematics

Introduction

Assessment, by which we mean all the procedures used to collect information on any aspect of the teaching and learning process, is an integral component of the *Math Thematics* curriculum. The Mathematical Sciences Education Board (1993) has described assessment as follows:

Assessment is the guidance system of education ... Assessment helps teachers and parents determine what students know and what they need to learn. It can play a powerful role in conveying clearly and directly how well students are learning ...

Informing parents and teachers is an important function, but assessment also serves another vital, though often unrecognized, purpose.

It is through our assessment that we communicate most clearly to students which activities and learning outcomes we value.

—David J. Clarke, Doug M. Clarke, and Charles J. Lovitt (1990)

The assessment component in *Math Thematics* provides a guidance system—a guidance system for teachers, for parents, and most importantly, for students.

Purposes of Assessment

The primary purpose of assessment is to improve learning. To achieve this goal, the *Math Thematics* assessment component is designed to be an integral part of the instructional process, rather than an add-on to it. Not only is assessment information drawn from instructional tasks, but the assessment tools themselves are designed to help students master concepts and develop skills.

The *Math Thematics* assessment component serves four major purposes:

- Monitoring student progress in problem solving, reasoning, and communication

A major goal of the *Math Thematics* curriculum is to develop each student's ability to solve problems, reason logically, and communicate ideas effectively. Making problem solving, reasoning, and communication a primary focus of assessment conveys the message that these are valued skills. But more importantly, the scales used for *Teacher Assessment* and *Student Self-Assessment* provide dynamic tools for helping students learn what they can do to improve in these areas.

- Assessing student proficiency in content areas

Assessment data are used to document students' understanding of mathematical content and processes, and to determine whether students have achieved the learner outcomes of the *Math Thematics* curriculum. The data are derived from multiple sources using a broad range of mathematical tasks.

- Helping teachers make instructional decisions

The assessment tools provide information teachers can use to decide what instruction is necessary to help students achieve the outcomes of the *Math Thematics* curriculum. The results of ongoing assessment may indicate a variety of needs such as reteaching concepts, reviewing or practicing skills, or presenting additional material using a different model or teaching technique.

- Documenting student progress for students, parents, and teachers

Assessment is about more than grades, but teachers are usually expected to translate assessment data into grades. Samples of student work gathered during assessment can provide an objective basis for determining student performance levels. Having a portfolio containing examples of a student's work can show growth over time. By comparing examples in the portfolio, you can clearly communicate to the student, parents, and other teachers the indicators of excellent work (A), good progress (B), developing concepts and skills (C), and minimally acceptable work (D).

Assessment Tools

The following assessment tools are incorporated into the *Math Thematics* curriculum.

Warm-Ups

Warm-Ups are short activities found in the annotated Teacher's Edition that provide systematic review of concepts and skills. *Warm-Ups* usually can be written on the board or projected with an overhead. They are often used for pre-assessment purposes to determine whether students have the prerequisite skills or knowledge for a section.

Embedded Questions

Because assessment in *Math Thematics* is an integral part of instruction, many assessment items are embedded in the instructional materials.

Discussion questions provide opportunities for students to check their understanding of a concept by sharing or generating ideas within their group or as a class. Mastery of the concept is not expected at this point, but teachers should monitor the discussions to check for misconceptions that may need to be corrected.

Checkpoints are questions or problems that are used by the teacher to check understanding of a concept or skill before students continue with the exploration. *Checkpoints* appear after students have explored a concept and when some level of mastery is expected. If students are not able to complete the problems correctly, re-teaching may be necessary.

Try This as a Class questions appear at points where direct instruction is needed to summarize key ideas or to bring closure to a line of inquiry. They are similar to *Discussion* questions, except that the teacher directs the discussion or activity and guides the learning. Not all *Try This as a Class* questions are used for assessment. Some are simply used to demonstrate a procedure or to pool data.

Some *Practice & Application Exercises* are designed to be used to assess whether students have learned specific concepts, procedures, and processes. These exercises, which may be used for instructional decision making and grading, are identified in the *Teacher's Resource Book* as embedded assessment exercises. They range from straightforward applications of concepts and procedures to open-ended questions that require students to recognize the appropriate mathematical content, choose an effective approach, and construct a response.

Reflecting on the Section exercises provide an opportunity for students to look back on the section as a whole and refine, describe, summarize, or extend the mathematical ideas they have explored. A *Reflecting* exercise may take the form of a *Discussion, Research, Oral Report, Journal,* or *Visual Thinking* question. Writing or talking about a concept helps students solidify their understanding of it. It may also help them make connections to other subject areas or among mathematical concepts. Students' responses to the *Reflecting* exercises should be considered for inclusion in their portfolios.

Extended Explorations (E^2s)

E^2s are extended problem solving activities. They are typically open-ended problems that apply a variety of mathematical concepts and may be solved in different ways. The solution often involves constructing a mathematical model for the situation. To solve the problem, students must define the problem, devise and carry out a plan for solving it, and prepare a presentation in which they explain and interpret their solution. Each E^2 may be assigned for completion in about a week's time. The solution is assessed using the *Teacher Assessment Scales* and *Student Self-Assessment Scales*. Solutions to some E^2s should be included in students' portfolios to document growth in problem solving, reasoning, and communication.

Module Projects

Each module contains a *Module Project* that provides an opportunity for students to apply mathematical concepts as they learn them. The project is related to the theme of the module, but may also require mathematical knowledge from earlier modules. Questions and activities throughout the module relate the project to the mathematical concepts being taught. At the end of the module, students prepare a report or presentation to complete the project. Some *Module Projects* should be included in students' portfolios to demonstrate their understanding of mathematical concepts as well as their ability to apply them.

Module Review and Assessment

Each module concludes with a set of questions that can be used to review and assess the content of the module. Additional assessment materials are provided in the *Teacher's Resource Book*. These include mid-module quizzes, module tests, Standardized Assessment, and Module Performance Assessment.

Portfolios

A student portfolio is a collection of representative samples of the student's work. It may include such things as assignments, answers to *Reflecting on the Section* exercises, solutions to E^2s, and *Module Projects*. Its purpose is to provide comprehensive documentation of the student's progress in, attitude toward, and understanding of mathematics over a period of time.

Using the Math Thematics Assessment Scales

PEANUTS reprinted by permission of United Feature Syndicate, Inc.

About the Math Thematics Assessment Scales

Sally's dilemma in the above cartoon is one that many students face. She has no idea what criteria were used to evaluate her work, and even worse, the assessment information she was given does not tell her anything about what she can do to improve!

The Math Thematics Assessment Scales are designed to help students answer the question "How can I improve my performance in problem solving, reasoning, and communications?" They provide a generalized rubric that defines the various dimensions of mathematical investigation. The scales are designed to be applied to open-ended questions, Module Projects, Reflecting on the Section exercises, and especially Extended Explorations (E^2s). Students are encouraged to write their solutions to these items using appropriate mathematical language and representations to communicate how they solved the problem, the decisions they made as they solved it, and any connections they made. Their work is assessed using five scales:

- Problem Solving
- Mathematical Language
- Representations
- Connections
- Presentation

The key to improving student performance is to actively involve them in assessing their own work. This is achieved through use of the Student Self-Assessment Scales. As students become familiar with the scales, they understand what they need to do to improve their problem solving, reasoning, and communication.

Teachers assess students' work using the same scales written from a teacher's point of view. The combination of student and teacher assessment provides important feedback to help students improve.

If used consistently, the Math Thematics Assessment Scales have the potential to raise the level of students' performance. However, you and your students will not master the use of the Math Thematics Assessment

Scales immediately. This is okay—the more work you and your students assess, the better and the more comfortable you will be with the assessment process.

As you work with the *Math Thematics* Assessment Scales, keep the following in mind:

- The scales are a powerful way for both you and your students to look at work.
- Learning to use the scales is like learning a new language. It requires time and patience.
- Students' higher-order thinking skills will improve as a result of using the *Math Thematics* Assessment Scales.
- Be flexible!

A copy of all the scales can be found on page 64 (*Teacher Assessment Scales*) and on page 65 (*Student Self-Assessment Scales*).

The following are descriptions of each scale.

The Problem Solving Scale

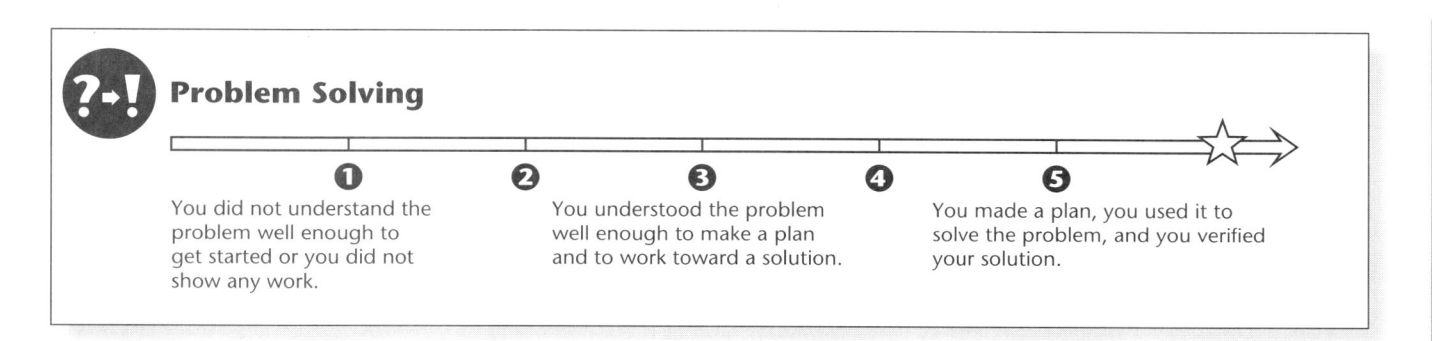

Problem Solving

① You did not understand the problem well enough to get started or you did not show any work.

②

③ You understood the problem well enough to make a plan and to work toward a solution.

④

⑤ You made a plan, you used it to solve the problem, and you verified your solution.

The *Problem Solving Scale* assesses the student's ability to select and use appropriate mathematical concepts and problem solving strategies (guess and check, make a model, look for a pattern, and so on) to solve a problem. The scale emphasizes and reinforces the steps in the *4-Step Approach to Solving Problems*—Understand the Problem, Make a Plan, Carry Out the Plan, and Look Back.

The *Teacher Assessment Scale* shown above gives the range of the criteria used to assess a student's work for problem solving. The following descriptions expand on the criteria.

Level 5: The student's approach worked and led to a correct solution.

The following are characteristics of a Level 5 solution:

- All the relevant information was used to solve the problem.
- The problem solving strategies, procedures, and mathematical concepts used were appropriate for the problem and were carried out completely.
- When strategies were only partially useful, the approach was modified successfully.
- The solution was checked for reasonableness.
- Other possible solutions were explored.
- The solution was verified through the use of a second approach or with a clear explanation of how the approach actually solved the problem.

Level 3: The student was able to make progress toward a solution.

The following are characteristics of a Level 3 solution:

- A workable plan was used, but the solution is incomplete or only solves part of the problem.
- The problem was only partially solved because some of the relevant data were not used.
- The mathematical procedures and problem solving strategies used were appropriate for the problem, but they were not carried out completely or they did not lead to a complete solution.
- The mathematical concepts chosen were appropriate but only partially solved the problem.

Professional Development Handbook

Level 1: The student did not understand the problem well enough to get started on a solution or did not show any work.

The following are characteristics of a Level 1 solution:

- There was no apparent plan for solving the problem or the solution was not related to the problem.
- Information was misinterpreted or irrelevant data were used.
- Problem solving strategies were used randomly or were not used at all.
- Incorrect or inappropriate mathematical procedures were used.
- The mathematical concepts chosen were not appropriate for the problem.

Levels 2 and 4 may be used to show performance that falls between the described levels. For example, a student may have used an appropriate approach and found a correct solution to the problem, but then stopped without checking the reasonableness of the solution or trying to verify it. This solution might be scored at Level 4 rather than Level 5. Similarly, a solution that has some of the characteristics of a Level 1 solution and some of a Level 3 solution might be scored at Level 2. The Star (☆) Level should only be used to indicate exceptional work.

The score on a scale is shown by filling it in with a marker up to the level number.

Questions Students Ask About the *Problem Solving Scale*

What is meant by a solution?

A solution includes your answer and all the work you did to get it. Sometimes it may be necessary to include an explanation of your approach and why you chose it.

What if I make a computation error? How does that affect my score?

The goal in problem solving is always to find an accurate solution, so you should make it a habit to check your work carefully. It is still possible, however, to get an incorrect answer because of a minor computational error. Depending on how serious the error is, this may lower your score one level on the *Problem Solving Scale*. The error will be noted at the bottom of the assessment sheet.

What does it mean to "verify my solution"?

The most common way to verify a solution is to solve it another way. For example, you could solve the problem using different problem solving strategies or a different approach and show that you get the same answer. Another way to verify your solution is by clearly explaining your plan and showing that it effectively solved the problem.

The Mathematical Language Scale

Mathematical Language

1. You did not use any mathematical vocabulary or symbols, or you did not use them correctly, or your use was not appropriate.
2.
3. You used appropriate mathematical language, but the way it was used was not always correct or other terms and symbols were needed.
4.
5. You used mathematical language that was correct and appropriate to make your meaning clear.

The *Mathematical Language Scale* assesses the student's use of mathematical vocabulary, notation, and symbols. The scale encourages consistent and accurate use of mathematical language.

Level 5: The student used mathematical language correctly and consistently. The language used was appropriate for the problem and it helped to simplify or clarify the solution.

The following are characteristics of a Level 5 solution:

- The mathematical language used was appropriate for the problem.
- The mathematical vocabulary and symbols were used consistently and accurately.
- The use of mathematical terms and symbols helped to communicate the solution.

Level 3: The student used appropriate mathematical vocabulary and symbols, but the usage was not always correct or additional terms and symbols could have been used to simplify the solution or make it clearer.

The following are characteristics of a Level 3 solution:

- The mathematical vocabulary and symbols chosen were appropriate for the problem but more could have been used.
- Appropriate mathematical terms and symbols were used, but they were not used consistently or there were minor errors in usage.

Level 1: The student did not use mathematical vocabulary or notation in the solution, or the terms and symbols used were inappropriate or used incorrectly.

The following are characteristics of a Level 1 solution:

- The use of mathematical terms and symbols the student should know would have helped to simplify or to clarify the solution, but none were used.
- Inappropriate mathematical language was used.
- Mathematical terms or symbols were used incorrectly or imprecisely.

Questions Students Ask About the *Mathematical Language Scale*

What is appropriate mathematical language?

You are using appropriate mathematical language if the terms and symbols you are using help to simplify your solution or to make it clearer. Using extraneous terms or symbols that do not relate to the problem or aid in the solution is inappropriate.

Does one mistake in language lower my score?

Usually, one error would not lower your score, especially if the other terms and symbols you used were appropriate and were used correctly.

Professional Development Handbook

The Representations Scale

Representations

① You did not use any representations such as equations, tables, graphs, or diagrams to help solve the problem or explain your solution.

②

③ You made appropriate representations to help solve the problem or help you explain your solution, but they were not always correct or other representations were needed.

④

⑤ You used appropriate and correct representations to solve the problem or explain your solution.

The *Representations Scale* assesses the student's use of graphs, tables, models, diagrams, and equations to solve problems. The *Representations Scale* looks specifically at whether the representations are accurate and appropriate.

Level 5: The student used representations that were accurate and appropriate for the problem. The representations helped to solve the problem or explain the solution.

The following are characteristics of a Level 5 solution:

- The representations used were appropriate for the problem.
- The representations helped to solve the problem or to communicate the solution.
- The representations were correct and accurate.

Level 3: The student used representations that were appropriate for the problem, but they were not always accurate or correct, and other representations could have been used to simplify the solution or to make it clearer.

The following are characteristics of a Level 3 solution:

- The representations used were appropriate for the problem, but additional representations were needed to solve the problem or to help communicate the solution.
- The representations were appropriate, but there were some errors in constructing or using the representations.

Level 1: The student did not use representations to help solve the problem or to explain the solution.

The following are characteristics of a Level 1 solution:

- The use of representations would have helped solve the problem or clarify the solution, but none were used.
- The representations used were inappropriate for the problem and did not help solve it or explain the solution.

Questions Students Ask About the *Representations Scale*

What makes a representation appropriate?

To be appropriate, a representation must accurately represent relevant information in the problem or help to organize the information. The representation should actually solve or help to solve the problem. For example, suppose the data in a problem could be displayed in a circle graph, but the graph does not solve the problem or give you a clue about how to solve it. Then it is inappropriate.

What makes a representation accurate?

A graph is accurate if the axes are labeled, the graph displays data that are relevant to the problem, the data are plotted accurately, the graph is titled correctly, and, if necessary, an accurate key is provided. A table, chart, diagram, or model is accurate if it is correctly labeled, it is well organized, and it accurately reflects information relevant to the problem.

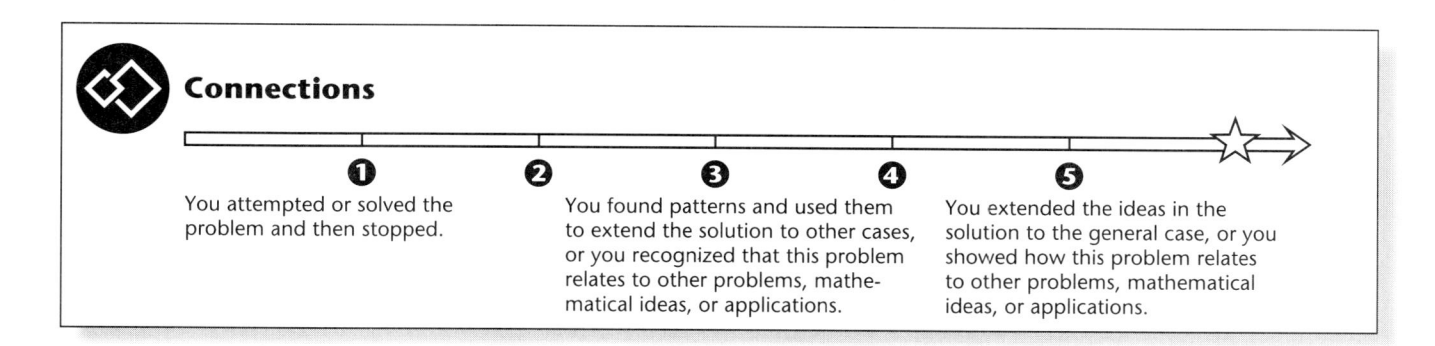

The Connections Scale

Connections

① You attempted or solved the problem and then stopped.

③ You found patterns and used them to extend the solution to other cases, or you recognized that this problem relates to other problems, mathematical ideas, or applications.

⑤ You extended the ideas in the solution to the general case, or you showed how this problem relates to other problems, mathematical ideas, or applications.

The *Connections Scale* assesses the student's ability to make connections within mathematics, to real-world situations, and to other disciplines. This scale emphasizes and reinforces the Look Back step in the *4-Step Approach to Solving Problems.*

This is the most difficult scale for students to understand and use. Because they often have limited mathematical knowledge and virtually no experience making connections, students' initial connections will be limited to recalling similar problems, finding and extending patterns, and relating the math to their everyday lives. To help students grow in this area, it is extremely important to continually encourage them and prompt them to look for and to make connections.

When extending solutions to the general case, many students lack the skills to express the general rule algebraically. Their extensions will involve descriptions of the patterns they found and may include a verbal rule. This is particularly true for sixth grade students. As students mature, their ability to use algebraic notation should increase, and they should become comfortable using it.

Level 5: The student generalized the solution or showed how the problem is related to other problems, mathematical ideas, or applications.

The following are characteristics of a Level 5 solution:

- The solution was extended to the general case.
- The solution was applied or interpreted in a real-world situation.
- The student clearly demonstrated how the problem is related to another mathematical concept or to another problem.

Level 3: The student recognized patterns and was able to use them to extend the solution to other cases of the same problem or recognized that the problem is related to other mathematical ideas, problems, or applications.

The following are characteristics of a Level 3 solution:

- The student found patterns that led to the solution but did not generalize the solution.
- The solution was extended to other cases of the same problem.

- Alternative solutions were explored.
- The student recognized that the problem is related to other problems, mathematical concepts, or applications but did not explain or illustrate the connection.

Level 1: The student solved the problem and stopped without looking back to see how the solution might be extended or generalized or how the problem relates to other problems, content, or applications.

The following are characteristics of a Level 1 solution:

- There are connections that the student should have recognized, but none were mentioned or explained in the solution.
- The solution does not indicate that the student looked for patterns that might be generalized.
- Alternative solutions were not recognized or were not pursued.
- The problem was not checked or examined from a different perspective.

ASSESSING

Professional Development Handbook

Questions Students Ask About the *Connections Scale*

What does it mean to extend my solution?

After you have solved a problem, you can extend it in many ways. One way is to solve the problem for different cases. For example, suppose a problem asked you to find the number of handshakes that would occur when five people shook hands exactly once. If you solved the problem for five people and then found the number of handshakes for six, seven, and eight people too, you have extended the solution. Another way to extend a problem is to write a general rule that can be used to find the number of handshakes for any number of people.

In Levels 3 and 5 on the Connections Scale, what is the difference between recognizing that the problem relates to other problems, mathematical ideas, or applications and showing that it does?

When you first begin making connections, you will discover that problems are related to other problems, mathematics, or applications. You might say "this is just like the handshake problem." In this case, you recognized the connection. When you show the connection, you will clearly link the problem, mathematics, or application with an explanation.

The Presentation Scale

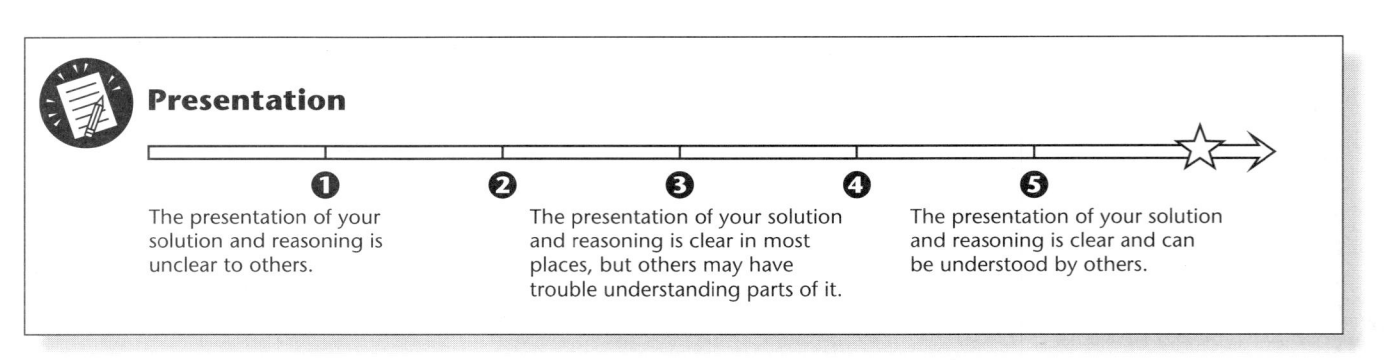

Presentation

❶ The presentation of your solution and reasoning is unclear to others.

❷

❸ The presentation of your solution and reasoning is clear in most places, but others may have trouble understanding parts of it.

❹

❺ The presentation of your solution and reasoning is clear and can be understood by others.

The *Presentation Scale* assesses the student's ability to reason logically and to communicate ideas effectively. This scale assesses why students did what they did to solve the problem. Evidence of reasoning is shown by making and testing conjectures, formulating models, explaining why, and gathering and presenting evidence. The differences between levels on the scale reflect both the correctness and the clarity of reasoning.

Level 5: The presentation clearly explains what the student did, why it was done, and how it solved the problem.

The following are characteristics of a Level 5 solution:

- The student's work was clear and focused. The details presented fit together and made sense.
- The presentation was well organized. One step followed from another.
- Strong supporting arguments were presented.
- All the important aspects of the problem and the relevant data were identified.
- Examples and counter-examples were included where appropriate.
- The solution is such that anyone who reads it will follow what was done, why it was done, and how the solution was obtained.

Level 3: The presentation explains what the student did and why it was done, but parts of the explanation are incorrect or are not clear.

The following are characteristics of a Level 3 solution:

- There is either an explanation or a clear inference of appropriate reasoning in the solution.
- Almost all of the reasoning is correct, but some of it may be unclear.

Math Thematics, Book 1

- There is evidence that unsuitable methods and incorrect solutions were eliminated.

Level 1: The presentation does not clearly explain or demonstrate what the student did or why it was done.

The following are characteristics of a Level 1 solution:

- The solution does not solve the question that was asked.
- There is no evidence of reasoned decision-making in the solution, or the solution indicates the possibility of reasoned decision-making, but the reader cannot be sure.
- The solution was organized in a haphazard or disjointed manner.
- The reasoning was incorrect.
- The solution does not contain an explanation of what was done and why, or the explanation is not understandable.

Questions Students Ask About the *Presentation Scale*

What does it mean to clearly explain my reasoning?

You must explain how you arrived at your solution and why you took each step you did. For example, if a student joined our class today and read your solution, would that student understand what you did and why you did it?

Do I always have to tell in words why I did what I did in order to score high on this scale?

It is possible that your work is organized so clearly that your reasoning can be inferred. However, it is helpful for you to explain what you did and why you did it. Some people think more clearly when they write things out, so writing helps them to clarify the situation and their thoughts.

Questions Teachers Ask About the *Assessment Scales*

What if the student and I do not agree on the assessment?

This is an excellent opportunity to discuss the differences between the assessments with the student. Comparing and contrasting the teacher and student assessments provides an important feedback loop that will lead to improved problem solving, reasoning, and communication.

Can the Math Thematics *Assessment Scales be used to assess problems that were solved as a group?*

Yes. Individual accountability is very important to the success of cooperative learning. So even if students work in a group to solve a problem, they should document the work individually. This individual documentation can be assessed using the assessment scales.

How can I tell if an exercise should be assessed with the Math Thematics *Assessment Scales?*

All *Extended Explorations* should be assessed using the assessment scales. Additional exercises that can be assessed with the scales are identified in the *Teacher's Resource Book*.

Will all the problems allow a student to score at the highest level on each scale?

No. Some problems have greater potential for certain scales than others. Sometimes students may not even be scored on a scale because the problem does not elicit the criteria for that scale.

If a problem is not scored on a scale, how will a grade be affected?

If a problem is not scored on a scale, the scale should not be counted when assigning the grade.

What if the student doesn't use the content I expected?

When solving problems, students should be encouraged to use any concepts they know. They should not be penalized for approaching the problem in a different way than the teacher expected.

Should I score students' earlier work more easily than later work?

No. The goal is to get students to improve so you should use a consistent scoring throughout the course.

When should I use Level 2, Level 4, and the Star (☆) Level as scores?

Levels 2 and 4 may be used to show performance that falls between the described levels. For example, a student may have used an appropriate approach and found a correct solution to the problem, but then stopped without checking the reasonableness of the solution or trying to verify it. This solution might be scored at Level 4 rather than Level 5. Similarly, a solution that has some of a Level 3 solution might be scored at Level 2. The Star (☆) Level should only be used to indicate exceptional work.

Professional Development Handbook

Name _____ Problem _____

TEACHER ASSESSMENT SCALES

☆ *The star indicates that you excelled in some way.*

❓➡❗ Problem Solving

① ② ③ ④ ⑤ ☆→

- **①** You did not understand the problem well enough to get started or you did not show any work.
- **③** You understood the problem well enough to make a plan and to work toward a solution.
- **⑤** You made a plan, you used it to solve the problem, and you verified your solution.

x^2 Mathematical Language

① ② ③ ④ ⑤ ☆→

- **①** You did not use any mathematical vocabulary or symbols, or you did not use them correctly, or your use was not appropriate.
- **③** You used appropriate mathematical language, but the way it was used was not always correct or other terms and symbols were needed.
- **⑤** You used mathematical language that was correct and appropriate to make your meaning clear.

Representations

① ② ③ ④ ⑤ ☆→

- **①** You did not use any representations such as equations, tables, graphs, or diagrams to help solve the problem or explain your solution.
- **③** You made appropriate representations to help solve the problem or help you explain your solution, but they were not always correct or other representations were needed.
- **⑤** You used appropriate and correct representations to solve the problem or explain your solution.

Connections

① ② ③ ④ ⑤ ☆→

- **①** You attempted or solved the problem and then stopped.
- **③** You found patterns and used them to extend the solution to other cases, or you recognized that this problem relates to other problems, mathematical ideas, or applications.
- **⑤** You extended the ideas in the solution to the general case, or you showed how this problem relates to other problems, mathematical ideas, or applications.

Presentation

① ② ③ ④ ⑤ ☆→

- **①** The presentation of your solution and reasoning is unclear to others.
- **③** The presentation of your solution and reasoning is clear in most places, but others may have trouble understanding parts of it.
- **⑤** The presentation of your solution and reasoning is clear and can be understood by others.

Content Used: _____ **Computational Errors:** Yes ___ No ___

Notes on Errors: _____

_____

64 *Math Thematics*, Book 1

Name _____   Problem _____

STUDENT SELF-ASSESSMENT SCALES

▨ If your score is in the shaded area, explain why on the back of this sheet and stop.

☆ The star indicates that you excelled in some way.

Problem Solving

1 — **2** — **3** — **4** — **5** — ☆→

- **1** I did not understand the problem well enough to get started or I did not show any work.
- **3** I understood the problem well enough to make a plan and to work toward a solution.
- **5** I made a plan, I used it to solve the problem, and I verified my solution.

Mathematical Language

1 — **2** — **3** — **4** — **5** — ☆→

- **1** I did not use any mathematical vocabulary or symbols, or I did not use them correctly, or my use was not appropriate.
- **3** I used appropriate mathematical language, but the way it was used was not always correct or other terms and symbols were needed.
- **5** I used mathematical language that was correct and appropriate to make my meaning clear.

Representations

1 — **2** — **3** — **4** — **5** — ☆→

- **1** I did not use any representations such as equations, tables, graphs, or diagrams to help solve the problem or explain my solution.
- **3** I made appropriate representations to help solve the problem or help me explain my solution, but they were not always correct or other representations were needed.
- **5** I used appropriate and correct representations to solve the problem or explain my solution.

Connections

1 — **2** — **3** — **4** — **5** — ☆→

- **1** I attempted or solved the problem and then stopped.
- **3** I found patterns and used them to extend the solution to other cases, or I recognized that this problem relates to other problems, mathematical ideas, or applications.
- **5** I extended the ideas in the solution to the general case, or I showed how this problem relates to other problems, mathematical ideas, or applications.

Presentation

1 — **2** — **3** — **4** — **5** — ☆→

- **1** The presentation of my solution and reasoning is unclear to others.
- **3** The presentation of my solution and reasoning is clear in most places, but others may have trouble understanding parts of it.
- **5** The presentation of my solution and reasoning is clear and can be understood by others.

ASSESSING

Professional Development Handbook

Managing Extended Explorations

ASSESSING

Estimating Animal Populations

(textbook page shown, Module 1 Extended Exploration, page 41)

SET UP You will need the Extended Exploration Labsheet.

The Situation
Since researchers have no way of controlling the movement of animals in the wild, it can be difficult to make accurate population counts. Often researchers can only make estimates from aerial photographs.

The Problem
Devise a method you can use to estimate the number of geese shown in *Geese Galore* on the labsheet without counting each goose. Then use your method to make an estimate.

Something to Think About
* What is your top-of-the-head guess about whether the number of geese shown is in the *tens*, *hundreds*, *thousands*, or *millions*?
* Have you ever estimated the size of a crowd at a movie or a sports event? If so, what methods did you use?

Present Your Results
Write a summary that clearly explains how you made your estimate of the number of geese in *Geese Galore*. Give your estimate and compare it with your top-of-the-head guess. Include an example of another situation where your method of estimation may be useful.

You'll assess your work on this and other *Extended Exploration* problems using one or more of the assessment scales shown on page 21. You learned how to use the mathematical language scale in Section 2. As you work through the rest of this module, you'll learn how to use the other assessment scales.

---

* Brainstorm possible approaches to the problem.

Answers to the questions in the shaded boxes are given on pages 78 and 79.

> 1. How might you introduce the E^2 shown above?
> 2. What approaches do you think would work best?
> 3. Solve the *Estimating Animal Populations* E^2.

Monitoring Student Progress

Students often do not fully comprehend a task until they start it. Thus, it is important to discuss the E^2 with students after they have had a day or two to think about it and to organize their ideas. You may also want to check with students, individually or as a class, one more time before the solution is due to monitor their progress.

If students have a difficult time getting started, you may want to:

* Make sure they have identified and collected the information needed to solve the problem.
* Give clues about appropriate problem solving strategies.
* Provide prompts about possible connections.

To help students organize their thinking, you may want to have them turn in an outline of what they plan to do before they venture off on their final product. You may also want to offer to look at students' work in progress.

Extended Explorations (E^2s) are open-ended, problem solving tasks designed to be completed independently. Many E^2s can be assigned to pairs or groups of students. An E^2 should take one or two weeks to complete.

Introducing the E^2

Some class time should be used to introduce and begin working on the E^2. This introduction should be done as a whole class.

* Discuss the due date. You have some flexibility as to when you assign E^2s. If you have five classes, do not have all the E^2s due the same day.
* Discuss the format for the E^2 solution. A sample form is shown on page 68.
* Make sure everyone understands the problem.
* Discuss what students know about the problem and what they do not know.

---

66 *Math Thematics*, Book 1

Before collecting the E^2, have students assess their own work using the *Student Self-Assessment Scales*. After they have assessed their work, you may want to:

- Have students share parts of their solutions with the class.
- Give students a chance to rework parts of their solution before turning it in.

4. Use the *Student Self-Assessment Scales* on page 65 and the descriptions of the scales on pages 56–63 to assess your work on *Estimating Animal Populations*.

Assessing Solutions

The E^2s are designed to be assessed using the *Math Thematics* Assessment Scales. The following are tips for assessing student work.

- Give yourself the same amount of time to evaluate the solutions as you gave the students to work on them.
- Look at the solution in the *Teacher's Resource Book* to get ideas about what scales to use and what a solution might contain. Use this information and the *Teacher Assessment Scales* to get an idea of what you might expect a student to do to score at each level on each scale.
- Read the entire solution before you begin to assess it.
- Read the entire solution again and refer to the descriptions of the scales on pages 58–65. As you become more familiar with the scales, you will not need to rely on the descriptions as often.
- Do not spend too much time deliberating over the scoring on a scale. Use your best judgment and move on. If you are not sure which level a solution scores at on a scale, score it between two levels.
- Be sure to record the mathematical content used and note any calculation errors on the bottom of the *Teacher Assessment Scales*.
- Students are not going to score high at first, but they will improve. The goal is that the final level reflect the student's highest potential.
- Students' solutions give you information about their conceptual understanding. When you recognize a misconception, have a conference with the student to clear it up.

5. Read over the solution to *Estimating Animal Populations* given in the *Teacher's Resource Book*. How would you score your solution now?

Grading Solutions

The reason for assessing an E^2 is to give students an indication of their current problem solving ability, how it has changed over time, and what they can do to continue to improve. Simply giving each solution a grade based on the total of the ratings on the scales does not achieve this goal. Instead, we recommend using scoring profiles like the ones on page 69 to help assign grades.

The line on a profile indicates the minimum level a student should score at on each scale for each response. The *Excellent* response is a composite of the abilities the *Math Thematics* curriculum strives to develop. A *Good* response reflects the primary objective of the curriculum; most students should eventually reach this level. The *Developing* response indicates progress toward an acceptable level. Anything below the *Developing* level reflects little effort or understanding.

Keep the following maxims in mind when converting scores into students' grades.

- Be flexible. The profiles are only suggestions. You must determine which procedure is best for converting your students' assessment data into grades.
- If you use the profiles, familiarize your students with them so they know how their grades were determined and what goal to work toward.

6. Use the *Teacher Assessment Scales* on page 64. Read, assess, and grade the students' sample work on pages 70 and 71.

Follow-Up

You will probably want to spend some class time allowing students to share their results and their strategies for solving the problem. You may want to use a bulletin board to display the solutions.

With the class as a whole you might want to:

- Discuss universal misunderstandings or misconceptions regarding a problem or a mathematical idea.
- Illustrate a variety of solutions, approaches, and connections.
- Highlight exceptional responses.

With the individual student, you may want to:

- Monitor individual growth on the scales.
- Compare the *Student Self-Assessment* with the *Teacher Assessment*.
- Give help or explanations regarding the student's individual solution.

Professional Development Handbook

Format for an E^2 Solution

Include the following three main headings in the write-up of your E^2 solution.

Problem Statement

Write out the problem in your own words.

Problem Solving Procedure

Include the following in this section of your write-up.

Work
- Show all of the work you did to solve the problem.
- Include any tables, charts, graphs, diagrams, models, drawings, or equations that helped you solve the problem.

Explanation
- Give a step-by-step explanation of what you did to solve the problem.
- Identify the problem solving strategies you used and explain why you chose them.
- Use correct mathematical vocabulary and symbols wherever they are needed.
- Explain any changes you made in your thinking.
- Explain why your answer makes sense.
- You may use tables, charts, graphs, diagrams, models, drawings, and equations to help explain your solution.
- Check your solution or verify it by solving the problem another way.

Connections
- Explain how this problem is like other problems you have solved.
- Explain how this problem relates to a real-world situation or another mathematical idea.
- Try to extend the solution to other problems that are like this one.
- Try to find a rule that will work for any case of the problem.

Conclusion

Include the following in this section of your write-up.

Answer
- Write your answer to the problem.
- Be sure you answered the question or questions in the problem and clearly described your solution.

Learning
- You may include more than one response.
- Summarize what you learned from solving the problem.

Sample Scoring Profiles

Excellent Response (A)

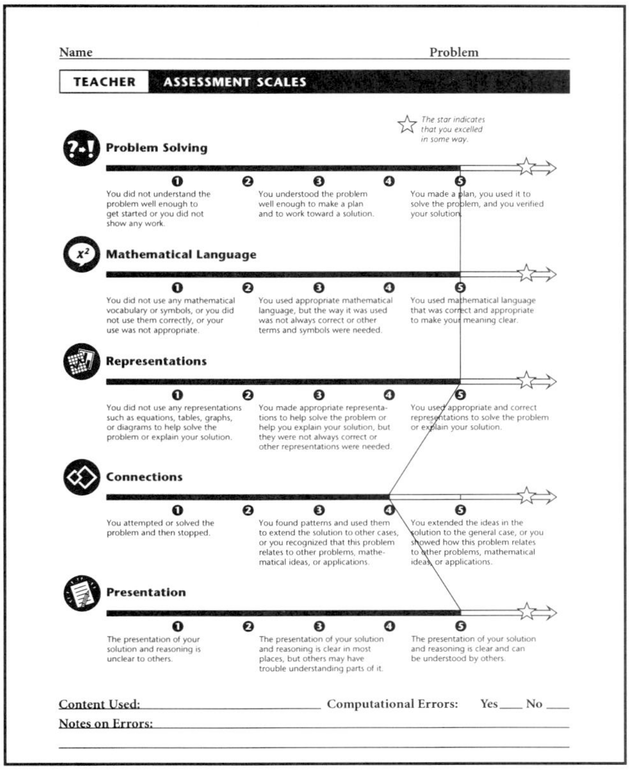
Name ____ Problem ____

TEACHER **ASSESSMENT SCALES**

The star indicates that you excelled in some way.

Problem Solving
1 You did not understand the problem well enough to get started or you did not show any work.
2
3 You understood the problem well enough to make a plan and to work toward a solution.
4
5 You made a plan, you used it to solve the problem, and you verified your solution.

Mathematical Language
1 You did not use any mathematical vocabulary or symbols, or you did not use them correctly, or your use was not appropriate.
2
3 You used appropriate mathematical language, but the way it was used was not always correct or other terms and symbols were needed.
4
5 You used mathematical language that was correct and appropriate to make your meaning clear.

Representations
1 You did not use any representations such as equations, tables, graphs, or diagrams to help solve the problem or explain your solution.
2
3 You made appropriate representations to help solve the problem or help you explain your solution, but they were not always correct or other representations were needed.
4
5 You used appropriate and correct representations to solve the problem or explain your solution.

Connections
1 You attempted or solved the problem and then stopped.
2
3 You found patterns and used them to extend the solution to other cases, or you recognized that this problem relates to other problems, mathematical ideas, or applications.
4
5 You extended the ideas in the solution to the general case, or you showed how this problem relates to other problems, mathematical ideas, or applications.

Presentation
1 The presentation of your solution and reasoning is unclear to others.
2
3 The presentation of your solution and reasoning is clear in most places, but others may have trouble understanding parts of it.
4
5 The presentation of your solution and reasoning is clear and can be understood by others.

Content Used: ____ Computational Errors: Yes ___ No ___
Notes on Errors: ____

Good Response (B)

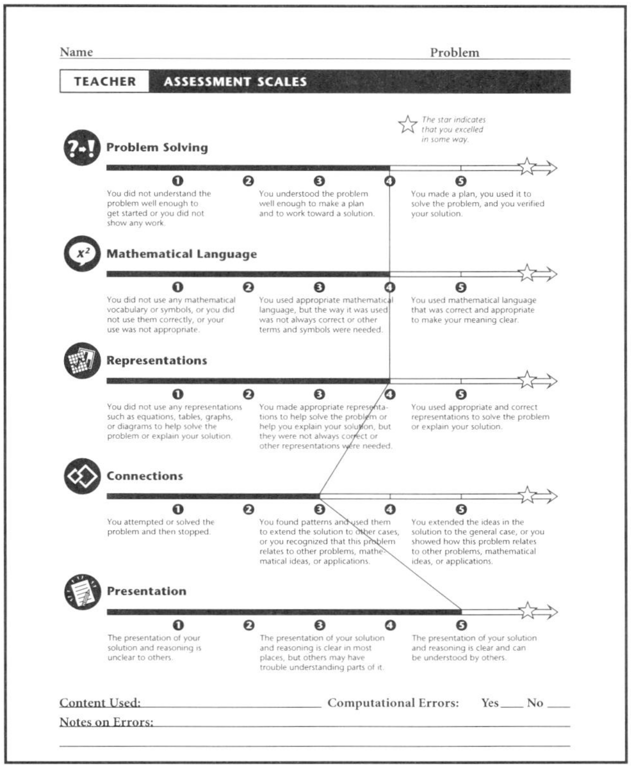
Name ____ Problem ____

TEACHER **ASSESSMENT SCALES**

The star indicates that you excelled in some way.

Problem Solving
1 You did not understand the problem well enough to get started or you did not show any work.
2
3 You understood the problem well enough to make a plan and to work toward a solution.
4
5 You made a plan, you used it to solve the problem, and you verified your solution.

Mathematical Language
1 You did not use any mathematical vocabulary or symbols, or you did not use them correctly, or your use was not appropriate.
2
3 You used appropriate mathematical language, but the way it was used was not always correct or other terms and symbols were needed.
4
5 You used mathematical language that was correct and appropriate to make your meaning clear.

Representations
1 You did not use any representations such as equations, tables, graphs, or diagrams to help solve the problem or explain your solution.
2
3 You made appropriate representations to help solve the problem or help you explain your solution, but they were not always correct or other representations were needed.
4
5 You used appropriate and correct representations to solve the problem or explain your solution.

Connections
1 You attempted or solved the problem and then stopped.
2
3 You found patterns and used them to extend the solution to other cases, or you recognized that this problem relates to other problems, mathematical ideas, or applications.
4
5 You extended the ideas in the solution to the general case, or you showed how this problem relates to other problems, mathematical ideas, or applications.

Presentation
1 The presentation of your solution and reasoning is unclear to others.
2
3 The presentation of your solution and reasoning is clear in most places, but others may have trouble understanding parts of it.
4
5 The presentation of your solution and reasoning is clear and can be understood by others.

Content Used: ____ Computational Errors: Yes ___ No ___
Notes on Errors: ____

ASSESSING

Developing Response (C)

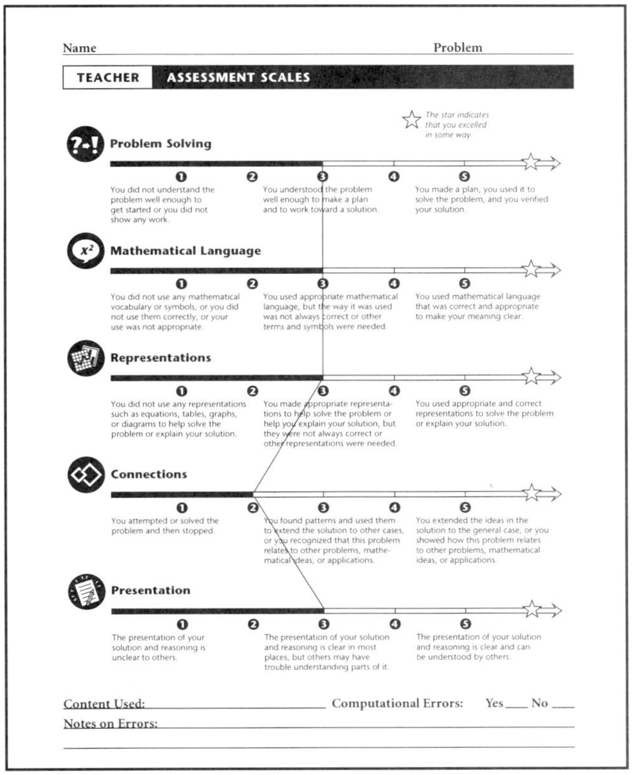
Name ____ Problem ____

TEACHER **ASSESSMENT SCALES**

The star indicates that you excelled in some way.

Problem Solving
1 You did not understand the problem well enough to get started or you did not show any work.
2
3 You understood the problem well enough to make a plan and to work toward a solution.
4
5 You made a plan, you used it to solve the problem, and you verified your solution.

Mathematical Language
1 You did not use any mathematical vocabulary or symbols, or you did not use them correctly, or your use was not appropriate.
2
3 You used appropriate mathematical language, but the way it was used was not always correct or other terms and symbols were needed.
4
5 You used mathematical language that was correct and appropriate to make your meaning clear.

Representations
1 You did not use any representations such as equations, tables, graphs, or diagrams to help solve the problem or explain your solution.
2
3 You made appropriate representations to help solve the problem or help you explain your solution, but they were not always correct or other representations were needed.
4
5 You used appropriate and correct representations to solve the problem or explain your solution.

Connections
1 You attempted or solved the problem and then stopped.
2
3 You found patterns and used them to extend the solution to other cases, or you recognized that this problem relates to other problems, mathematical ideas, or applications.
4
5 You extended the ideas in the solution to the general case, or you showed how this problem relates to other problems, mathematical ideas, or applications.

Presentation
1 The presentation of your solution and reasoning is unclear to others.
2
3 The presentation of your solution and reasoning is clear in most places, but others may have trouble understanding parts of it.
4
5 The presentation of your solution and reasoning is clear and can be understood by others.

Content Used: ____ Computational Errors: Yes ___ No ___
Notes on Errors: ____

Student Sample 1: Michael's Solution

In order to estimate the number of geese in the picture, you can draw a grid using horizontal lines only. By counting the number of geese in one section and then multiplying that number times the total number of sections, my estimation came out to be 663.

17
16
15
14
13
12
11
10
9 [*]   39 × 17 = 663
8
7
6
5
4
3
2
1

Key
* = a goose
9 = the section of geese I counted

I noticed this type of reasoning would work on finding the population density of a city. A city, in general, has more people living towards the center of it. As you move outward, you get into small suburbs and finally farmland or countryside. (At least here in Oklahoma.) The population decreases and houses are spread farther apart.

Student Sample 2: Annie's Solution

Problem Statement There is a large flock of geese. Don't count each goose, but try to figure out how many geese there are.

Problem Solving Approach I used a few approaches to solving the problem of estimating how many geese there were in the flock. First, I cut out a 2 in. by 2 in. square. Then I traced around the square in the center of the geese picture. I counted how many geese were in the square and multiplied it by 12.75. My product was 12.75 × 66 or about 840. I thought this might be too big because there seem to be more geese in the middle than in other places.

For the second approach, I drew one line vertically down the middle of the picture and one line horizontally across the middle of the picture. I counted the number of geese that were "hit" by the two lines. I multiplied those numbers and got my product which was 15 × 36 or 540. I took the two answers which were 840 and 540 and averaged them out which came to a total of 690.

First Approach   Second Approach
                       3.25 in.

                                   The reason why I did the problem the way I did
                                   is because it seemed pretty easy and it was. I
                                   had fun doing this paper so I guess the way I did
                   4.5 in.   the problem was ok. The strategies that I used
                                   were making a chart and drawing a picture. The
                                   only problem I had along the way was that I
                                   couldn't find out a way to do the problem. I tried
                                   many ways, but they were too complicated.

Conclusion What I found out when figuring out my solution is that there isn't a right answer when estimating and that I don't want to count tiny geese again.

I thought this problem was like estimating how many pennies or jelly beans there are in a jar or estimating how many rocks there are in a yard. I think you could use this problem in real life if you were a bird watcher looking at a flock. You might want to know how many birds were in the flock. You might use it in real life if you had to lay tile down on a huge room. You could lay a few and estimate how many more tiles you would need.

Approaches	Total
I drew a 2 in. by 2 in. square in the center of the geese sheet. Then I counted all of the geese in the square and multiplied it by 12.75.	840
I counted the amount of geese that were "hit" by a line drawn vertically down the middle of the geese sheet. Then I counted the number of geese that were "hit" by a line drawn horizontally. I multiplied the two numbers.	540
The average of the two.	690

Professional Development Handbook

Using Portfolios

Why Portfolios?

A portfolio is a showcase for student work, a place where many types of assignments, projects, reports, and writings can be collected. Progress in, attitudes toward, and understanding of mathematics can be seen in a comprehensive way. The collection exemplifies the goals of the NCTM Evaluation Standards and shows much more than will a single test.

—*Mathematics Assessment,*
NCTM (1991)

Portfolios are a means of assessing students' progress over time. They allow the teacher to focus on a student's collected work rather than on the work of all students on a single activity. Because they provide students with an opportunity for reflection and goal-setting, portfolios are valuable self-assessment tools. By providing tangible evidence of what students have achieved, portfolios help to instill a sense of pride and accomplishment in students and provide very useful tools for communicating with students, parents, and other teachers.

Creating Portfolios

The *Math Thematics* curriculum recognizes the importance of maintaining student portfolios, but understands that there is no single format that will meet the needs of all teachers and all schools using the curriculum. What follows is one possible model.

A portfolio is created cooperatively by the student and the teacher. Work selected for inclusion in the portfolio by the teacher or the student must be accompanied by a *Portfolio Entry Cover Sheet* completed by the student. The cover sheet describes why the piece was chosen, how it reflects the student's understanding of the mathematics content, and any other reflections the student may have. At any time, the student may improve the work. When the student improves a piece, the *Portfolio Entry Cover Sheet* must include what portions were changed and why the student decided to improve the piece.

To create the portfolio, the student should have two folders. In one folder, the student should keep all of the work during a grading period. The student can then look at the work and decide which pieces should be included in the portfolio. The teacher may suggest some pieces to be included. There may also be times when a teacher tells all students to include a particular piece in their portfolios. The student is responsible for organizing the work in the portfolio with suggestions given by the teacher. Some suggestions on what may be included in the portfolio are given on the next page.

Contents of a Portfolio

Your portfolio represents your work as a mathematics student. It should be something that you would be proud to show other students, teachers, and parents. It must be organized and neat. The portfolio should show the progress you make over a period of time. The following items must be included in your portfolio.

Table of Contents: The first page of your portfolio (not including the cover) should be the *Table of Contents*. The work in your portfolio should be numbered in the same order as in your *Table of Contents*.

Letter to the Reader: The *Letter to the Reader* should give a brief description of how the portfolio reflects your understanding of mathematics and brief descriptions of the pieces in the portfolio.

Self-Assessment Form: The *Self-Assessment Form* gives you the opportunity to reflect on your progress. You may also list any important goals you might have for the next grading period.

Portfolio Entry Cover Sheet: A *Portfolio Entry Cover Sheet* should accompany each piece going into your portfolio.

Work: The work included in your portfolio will vary. Individual pieces may include: *Extended Explorations* (E^2s), *Module Projects*, home or class assignments, tests and quizzes, work from a section, and *Reflecting on the Section* exercises.

Mathematical Autobiography: Your *Mathematical Autobiography* gives you the opportunity to reflect on your past mathematical experiences and attitudes. It should be completed at the beginning of the year.

Attitude Survey: In the *Attitude Survey*, you reflect on your attitudes about mathematics and what improvements could be made in the class.

Portfolio Summary: The *Portfolio Summary* should be included at the end of your portfolio. In it, you should summarize your progress. You also have the opportunity to identify particular goals you may have for the future.

Organizing Your Work

Save all your work in the work folder. At any time, you may choose a piece of work to include in your portfolio. All work going into your work folder must be dated and include your name. Keep the following in your work folder:

- All tests and quizzes.
- All class work and homework assignments.
- All E^2s and *Self-Assessment Forms*.
- *Module Projects*.
- Any other assignment that you needed to complete.

You may improve any piece of work you have completed. When you do, include a written description of what you improved and why you improved the work. This will be helpful if you decide to include the piece in your portfolio.

You may begin creating the actual portfolio at any time by selecting pieces you feel best reflect your work. Each piece must include a *Portfolio Entry Cover Sheet*.

ASSESSING

Professional Development Handbook

ASSESSING

Name _____ Date _____

Portfolio Entry Cover Sheet

I am including this in my portfolio because:

As you review this work, I hope you will notice:

(If this piece needs revision, you must explain how you would improve it and/or what the mistakes were. If you still have difficulties with the mathematics, you need to attach an explanation to this sheet.)

Name _____ Date _____

Self-Assessment Form

For each of the following statements, check the response that best describes your ideas about your work in this grading period.

Problem Solving

	Usually	Sometimes	Rarely
I am able to read the problem successfully and understand what it is about.	☐	☐	☐
I am able to develop a plan and choose a strategy to solve the problem.	☐	☐	☐
I am able to apply problem solving strategies in working through the problem.	☐	☐	☐
I often look back over my work to see that I have answered the questions accurately and completely.	☐	☐	☐

Mathematical Communication

	Usually	Sometimes	Rarely
I use mathematical vocabulary in talking and writing about mathematics.	☐	☐	☐
I feel confident when reading and writing mathematical symbols.	☐	☐	☐
I regularly use and understand models, diagrams, tables, and graphs.	☐	☐	☐

Mathematical Reasoning

	Usually	Sometimes	Rarely
I am able to explain and support my thoughts and conclusions about mathematical ideas.	☐	☐	☐
I am able to understand other people's mathematical thoughts and explanations.	☐	☐	☐

Mathematical Connections

	Usually	Sometimes	Rarely
Remembering what I've already learned helps me understand new math topics.	☐	☐	☐

These are the important things I want to work on:

1.
2.
3.

Math Thematics, Book 1

Name _____ Date _____

Mathematical Autobiography

Describe some math experiences that you remember from past school years. Be sure to include your best and worst moments as a mathematics student last year. Also include what expectations you have for yourself this year in math class.

Name _____ Date _____

Portfolio Summary

Write a summary of what you have learned in math class. Be sure to include what you have learned about yourself as a mathematics student and what goals you have for the next grading period.

Name _____ Date _____

Attitude Survey

1. Name two or three of the most important or most interesting things you have learned in math class. Explain why they were interesting or important.

2. Name at least one area of mathematics with which you still need help.

3. How do you feel at this moment about math class? (Circle all that apply. If needed, fill in the blank with another adjective you feel applies.)

interested   successful   excited   happy   relaxed

confused   worried   rushed   frustrated

_____

4. Name one way you can improve math class. Also suggest one way the class as a whole could be improved.

ASSESSING

Professional Development Handbook   **75**

Math Thematics Assessment Summary

Assessment in *Math Thematics* utilizes a variety of tools: *Warm-Ups*, embedded questions, *Extended Explorations* (E^2s), *Module Review and Assessments*, *Module Projects*, and portfolios. The assessment component is designed to be used by teachers to assess student proficiency in content areas, to monitor student progress in problem solving, reasoning, and communication, to make instructional decisions, and for grading. The assessment component is also designed specifically to be used by students for self-assessment. The recommended uses of the assessment tools are summarized in the following table.

Tool	Used to Assess	Who Assesses	Examples from Book 1 Module 3	Purpose
Embedded Questions: *Discussion*	• understanding of a concept	• student	Question 7, p. 184	• self-assessment
Checkpoint	• mastery of a skill	• teacher	Question 5, p. 184 Question 8, p. 184	• assess student proficiency in content area • make instructional decisions
Try This as a Class	• understanding of a concept or an algorithm • application of concepts and skills	• student • teacher	Question 14, p. 187	• self-assessment • assess student proficiency in content area • make instructional decisions
Practice & Application Exercises (identified in the *Teacher's Resource Book*)	• understanding of a concept • mastery of a skill • application of concepts and skills	• teacher	Exercises 1, 2, 6, and 7, p. 189	• assess student proficiency in content area • make instructional decisions • monitor student progress in problem solving, reasoning, and communication • grading
Reflecting on the Section Questions Oral Report Journal Research Visual Thinking Discussion	• understanding of a concept • application of concepts and skills • problem solving, reasoning, and communication	• student • teacher • the *Teacher Assessment Scales* and *Student Self-Assessment Scales* can be used on open-ended items (optional)	Exercise 52, p. 179 Exercise 22, p. 192 Exercise 29, p. 205 Exercise 33, p. 216 Exercise 26, p. 226	• self-assessment • monitor student progress in problem solving, reasoning and communication • grading

Tool	Used to Assess	Who Assesses	Examples from Book 1 Module 3	Purpose
Warm-Ups	• prerequisite skills and concepts for a Section	• teacher	See Teacher's Edition, pp. 158, 171, 182, 195, 207, and 218.	• assess student proficiency in content areas • make instructional decisions
Extended Explorations (E²s)	• problem solving, reasoning, and communication • application of concepts and skills	• student using the *Student Self-Assessment Scales* • teacher using the *Teacher Assessment Scales*	*What a Zoo!*, p. 194	• self-assessment • monitor student progress in problem solving, reasoning, and communication • grading
Module Projects	• mastery of specific content • problem solving, reasoning, and communication • application of concepts and skills	• student using the *Student Self-Assessment Scales* • teacher • teacher using the *Teacher Assessment Scales* (optional)	See pp. 180, 192, 216, and 229.	• self-assessment • monitor student progress in problem solving, reasoning, and communication • grading
Module Review and Assessment	• mastery of specific content • problem solving, reasoning, and communication • application of concepts and skills	• teacher • the *Teacher Assessment Scales* and *Student Self-Assessment Scales* can be used on open-ended items (optional)	See pp. 230, and 231.	• assess student proficiency in content areas • monitor student progress in problem solving, reasoning, and communication • make instructional decisions • grading
Portfolios	• growth over time and perseverance in problem solving, reasoning, and communication	• student • teacher		• self-assessment • assess student proficiency in content areas • monitor student progress in problem solving, reasoning, and communication • reporting to parents

Answers to Assessment Questions

This section contains answers to the questions in the **Managing Extended Explorations** section.

1. *How might you introduce the* Estimating Animal Populations E^2?

You could begin by having students share their ideas about why wildlife biologists might want to know the population of a particular kind of animal in a region, the methods researchers might use to count the animals, and what problems they might encounter taking a count. This discussion could provide a lead into estimating the number from a photograph. After introducing the problem, discuss the due date and the format students should use for their presentation.

2. *What approaches do you think would work best?*

The best approach to the problem may be to randomly select a small region on the photo and count the geese in that region. The ratio of the area of the photo to the area of the small region can then be used to predict the number of geese in the photo. If this process is repeated 3 or 4 times, the mean of the estimates from the individual samples should give a good estimate of the number of geese in the photo.

Students often use some variation of the "count the geese in a smaller region" method to make their estimates, but they usually do not select the regions randomly or repeat the sampling to verify their result or to find an average.

6. *Read, assess, and grade the students' sample work on pages 70 and 71.*

Michael's Solution

Michael's solution would score at Level 4 on the *Problem Solving Scale*. He understood the problem well enough to make a plan and find a solution, but he did not attempt to verify his solution or check that it was reasonable.

This E^2 does not provide an opportunity for students to use much mathematical vocabulary, so you may decide not to score their solutions on the *Mathematical Language Scale*. Michael's solution would score at Level 3 on the scale. He did use appropriate terms like *grid* and *multiplying* correctly, but he could have used other mathematical terms to describe his estimate (the *product*) and the grid (*rectangular* sections). He also used the term *line* when he meant *segment*. You could also legitimately score this solution at Level 1 since, with the exception of *multiplying*, no mathematical language was used, or at Level 5 because the other uses indicated would not have made the solution any clearer.

Michael's solution would score at Level 5 on the *Representations Scale*. The equation and drawing that he used were appropriate and helped explain his solution.

Michael *explained* how his method of solving the problem is related to the problem of estimating the population of a city. His explanation of the connections could have been clearer, so his solution would score at Level 4 on the *Connections Scale*.

Michael's presentation of his solution can be understood by others, but he did not clearly explain his reasoning. Why is it appropriate to estimate the number of geese by multiplying the number in one section by the number of sections? Would this method work for any section (in particular, Sections 1 or 17)? How does he know his estimate is reasonable? Because his reasoning is not clear or necessarily correct, his solution would score at Level 3 on the *Presentation Scale*.

Michael's solution would be considered a **Good Response**. He is a little lower on the *Mathematical Language Scale* than shown on the Good Response Profile, but this problem did not provide much opportunity to use mathematical terms or symbols. He is also lower than the Profile on the *Presentation Scale*, but this is the first E^2 in the book, so that is not unusual. Also, his high score on the *Representations Scale* tends to balance this out.

Annie's Solution

Annie's solution would score at Level 5 on the *Problem Solving Scale*. Not only did she understand the problem well enough to make a plan and find a solution, but she checked that it was reasonable when she decided that the estimate was too high and used a new approach to find another estimate. She apparently decided the second estimate was too low and averaged the results to get her final estimate.

Annie's solution would score at Level 4 on the *Mathematical Language Scale*. She used terms like *square, multiplied, product,* and *averaged* where they were appropriate, and she used them correctly. She used *line* instead of *segment* and could have used *area* if she had explained why she multiplied by 12.75.

Annie's solution would score at Level 5 on the *Representations Scale*. The drawings and table she used were appropriate and helped explain her solution.

Annie *recognized* that this problem is related to other types of problems but did not try to explain how they are related. It would also have been nice if Annie had explained how her second approach relates to her understanding of multiplication (the array model). Her solution would score at Level 3 on the *Connections Scale*.

Annie did not explain how she found the 12.75 or why she would multiply the number of geese in the square by it. Annie also needed to explain whether her second estimate was reasonable or not and why she decided to average the two estimates. Other than this, the presentation of her solution is clear and can be understood by others. She also did not recognize or did not explain the need to do a random sample with both of her methods. Her solution would score at Level 4 on the *Presentation Scale*.

Annie's solution would be considered an **Excellent Response**, especially for her first E^2. She is a little lower on the *Mathematical Language Scale* than shown on the Excellent Response Profile, but considering that this problem did not provide much opportunity to use mathematical terms or symbols she did very well. She is also lower than the Profile on the *Connections* and *Presentation Scales*, but this is a difficult problem for which to find connections and her solution did display considerable thought and originality.

Implementing the Math Thematics Curriculum

Communicating with Parents

Middle school is a time of dramatic changes for young adolescents. Students often need the guidance and support of adults, particularly their parents. But parents, too, need guidance. Studies show that parents become increasingly less involved with their child's school, teachers, and subject matter once their children reach middle school. In addition, "parents of children in middle grades received less information and guidance precisely at the time when they needed more..." (Rutherford, 1990).

Research has shown that students perform better when there is a strong parent involvement program that includes communicating with parents and other family members on a regular basis (Cavazos, 1989). Communication can be achieved through letters, newsletters, individual conferences, and workshops. We recommend that you use a variety of methods to reach parents, but adjust the content or delivery to best suit your community.

Letter to Parents

Most parents remember mathematics classes as hours spent doing endless arithmetic problems. Although this teaching strategy is viable for a small number of students, it does not address the learning styles of most students, nor the intellectual needs of our society. Before we can expect the support of parents, we need to explain the changes in mathematics education. It is important to warn parents that their children will be exploring mathematics using cooperative learning and manipulatives. Most parents will not be familiar with these tools or the idea of discovery learning. One way to apprise parents is to send out a general letter informing them about the text their students will be using and the philosophy of the curriculum. We suggest using a letter similar to the one below.

Dear Family Members,

This year we'll be using the *Middle Grades Math Thematics* curriculum. This curriculum is designed to help all students develop their mathematical understanding and ability. The materials stress not only key mathematical skills, but also the importance of problem solving, reasoning, and critical thinking. One component of this approach is that students will spend time discussing and writing about mathematics.

Math Thematics uses a variety of instructional techniques including discovery learning and real-world problems to motivate students. For example, students explore the size and mass of dinosaurs and learn to create statistical graphs to categorize them. Because the program allows students to discover the mathematics, you will see few step-by-step procedures. This does not mean that students are completely on their own. There are many examples and pages of the text that will help you and your child identify the content that is most important. These special pages include:

- *Key Concepts* pages which summarize what students have learned in each section.
- *Student Resource* pages which appear throughout the book and give detailed guidance on various mathematical skills, such as choosing the scale on a graph or constructing a perpendicular bisector.
- The *Toolbox* at the end of the book which helps students review essential skills they need this year but may have forgotten.

You should expect to see homework assignments at least three nights each week. Some of these problems reinforce skills while others require more thought and effort. As part of your child's homework, you may be asked to help conduct an experiment, answer questions for a survey, or play a math game.

I have planned a **Math for Parents** meeting to familiarize you with the text and to answer questions. The first session will be held on (__date__). Additional information about this parent session will be sent home with your child.

Sincerely,

Newsletters

For each module of *Math Thematics* the *Teacher's Resource Book* includes a Math Gazette. This newsletter informs parents about the mathematics, activities, and real-world situations their children will explore over the next month. Questions are provided to help parents discuss the mathematics and themes with their child. The newsletter also lists several activities parents can do at home with their child, and it describes the *Extended Explorations (E²)*. We encourage you to copy and distribute these newsletters on a regular basis. A sample newsletter for Module 3 of Book 1 is shown below.

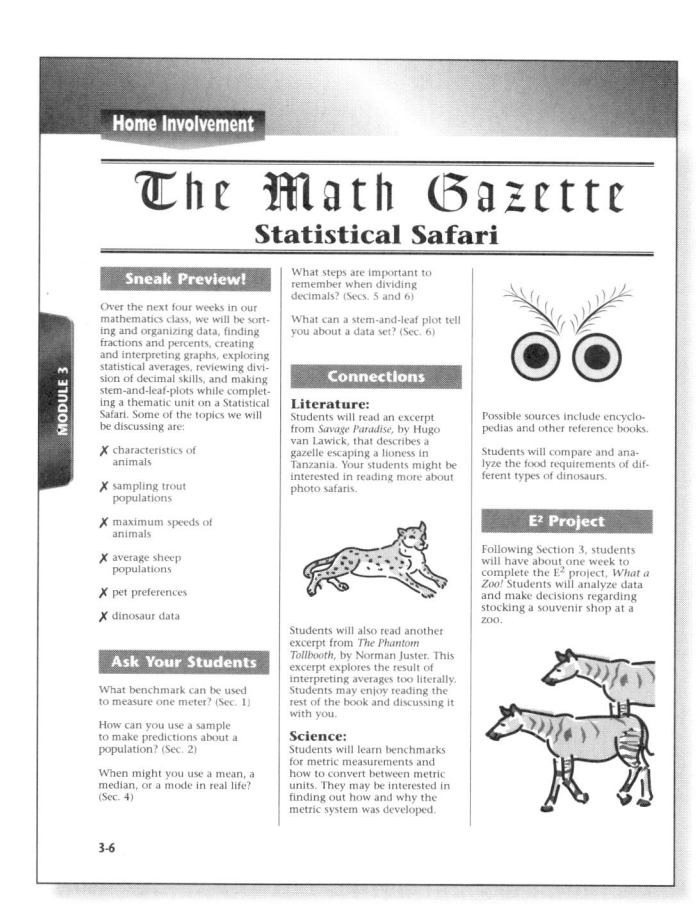

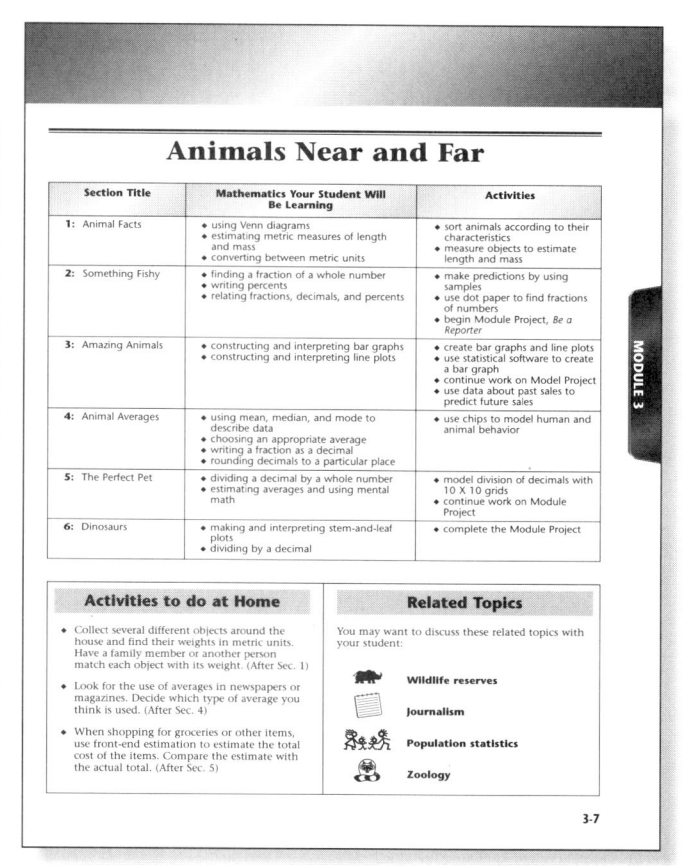

Conferences

Parent-teacher conferences are one way for teachers to learn more about their students. Parents usually enjoy talking about the interests and strengths of their children. As a teacher, you can find out how your students feel about school and mathematics. This communication can help parents feel involved in their child's schooling. By creating a team atmosphere, you can later enlist the help and support of parents.

If the parent has attended the **Math for Parents** meetings, he or she is familiar with your assessment philosophy. If not, you may need to briefly explain how you grade the embedded assessment exercises, journal entries, module assessment, and *Module Projects*.

Parents should have a chance to see their child's work. The assessment shown should be both traditional and authentic. For more information on assessment, see pages 54–79 in this handbook.

Since *Math Thematics* includes many opportunities for students to explore open-ended problems, you may want to create a bulletin board or class book with sample student work. The *Module Projects* and *Extended Explorations (E²s)* provide excellent material for display centers.

Professional Development Handbook

Math for Parents

The **Math for Parents** meetings are opportunities to discuss the concerns of parents and to explore the pedagogical approaches in *Math Thematics*. Your department may want to hold one meeting or several depending on the needs of your community. For example, four meetings in a year could be scheduled as follows:

- Meeting #1: two weeks into the school year
- Meeting #2: one month into the school year
- Meeting #3: half way through the school year
- Meeting #4: at the end of the school year

The 4th meeting would be an orientation for parents of 5th grade students. We suggest that the entire mathematics department organize and participate in these meetings. This ensures that all parents hear the same message.

The best way to introduce the philosophy of *Math Thematics* is to have parents work in cooperative groups to complete an activity. The activity should be one that students will complete this year. When discussing assessment, have parents try an E^2 and self-assess their work using the *Math Thematics* Assessment Scales.

Because there are many issues that can be discussed in these meetings, we have outlined the first two meetings in the tables below and on the following page. Other issues, such as pre-algebra or technology, may come up in one of these meetings however, so be prepared to address these concerns.

Calling All Parents!

Math for Parents is a great way to find out what your son or daughter is doing in math class.

Please join us from 7:00 - 8:30 p.m. on Wednesday, October 14.

Questions?
Call Mr. Jones, Mrs. Chin, or Mr. Gonzalez at 555-1234.

Meeting #1

Agenda	Discussion Points	Materials Needed
Overview of *Math Thematics*	• The goal of *Math Thematics* is to help all students develop their mathematical ability. • There are provisions for advanced students and learning disabled students. • This is a complete curriculum, not supplementary material. • It is theme-based to get kids interested in the mathematics. • Many factors have contributed to the changes in math education: technology, industry and the economy, and research on learning and adolescents.	Philosophy, pp. 2–3 Organization of Material in Student Book, p. 4 Why Change Mathematics Education?, p. 9
Introduction to the hands-on, discovery philosophy	• Students progress from a concrete model to pictures. Then they go from pictures to symbols. Eventually, all students will be at symbolic level, but it can take time. • This is a basic introduction to integers. Mastery is not expected at this level. • Manipulatives and other tools are used to make the ideas more real for students. Many students learn best by working with objects rather than by just pencil-and-paper activities. • Not all students need manipulatives, but most will understand the concepts better by using them.	From the student book: Integer activity, pp. 526–529
Helping with homework	• Encouraging children is the best way to help. Saying "I know you can do this!" is a great motivator. • *Key Concepts*, *Toolbox*, *Student Resource* pages, and *For Help* boxes are provided to help students and parents review concepts. • If possible, allow parents and students to call you at home if they have questions.	From the student book: Key Concepts, p. 533 Toolbox, p. 589

Meeting #2

Agenda	Discussion Points	Materials Needed
Cooperative learning	• Students need to interact with each other and be active in their learning process.	*Cooperative Learning* and *A Look at Middle Grade Students*, see below
Learning the "basics"	• The "basics" are an important part of every child's education. Each book in *Math Thematics* explores and reviews the basic concepts of computation, mental math, and estimation. • Number ideas are taught in each of the eight modules in Book 1. • Both the customary and metric systems for measuring are taught.	Module Themes and Content with NCTM Standards, pp. 5–8
Assessment	• Assessment is an integral part of the instructional process. • The assessment tools include embedded assessment, journal entries, module assessment, *Module Projects*, and *Extended Explorations* (E^2s).	E^2: Add-a-Square, pencils, colored tiles, graph paper, Student Self-Assessment Scales

These sample overheads can be used in the second **Math for Parents** meeting.

Cooperative Learning

Cooperative learning has been shown to help students to learn course material faster and retain it longer and to develop critical reasoning power more rapidly than working alone.

—Carnegie Council on Adolescent Development, TURNING POINTS (1989)

Cooperative learning in the mathematics classroom can help students

- communicate about mathematics,
- discover mathematical concepts, and
- develop a deeper understanding of mathematics.

A Look at Middle Grade Students

Diversity
Middle grade students have widely differing interests and social concerns. Students need to see a variety of real-world topics that relate to the mathematics content. Some of these topics should address social issues of concern to students at this age, such as recycling or endangered animals.

Socially
Students in the middle grades need to learn to interact with their peers. They often look to adults as models for these social skills. Cooperative learning is one way to structure positive interaction in a classroom.

Physically
These students are experiencing rapid physical growth which affects their attention span and energy level. Middle grade students need to be physically involved in their learning. This can take place with the use of manipulatives or other hands-on activities.

Academically
Students at this age begin the transition from concrete to abstract thinking. They need to use hands-on models, see pictures of the models, and learn to express their solutions using symbols.

Cooperative Learning

There are three ways to organize how students will interact in a classroom (Bennett, 1991).

Competitive Learning

IT'S ME AGAINST YOU!

Individualistic Learning

I'M ON MY OWN...

Cooperative Learning

WE ARE IN THIS TOGETHER!

Researchers have looked at the effect of these three approaches on student achievement. In reports by Johnson and Johnson (1984) and others, teachers that use cooperative learning found that:

- Cooperative learning produces higher levels of achievement than competitive or individualistic learning.
- The discussion that takes place in cooperative learning groups promotes discovery and the development of higher quality cognitive strategies.
- Conflicts of ideas or opinions can increase motivation, resulting in higher achievement and retention of the content, and produce a greater depth of understanding.
- The discussion in groups helps store the information in long-term memory, generally increasing achievement.
- Understanding and adjusting for special needs students is taken on by the students in the group.

Isn't It Just Group Learning?

Is cooperative learning simply placing students in groups and letting them work together? The answer is "no." There is much more to cooperative learning than organizing students into groups. Without training on what is expected during group work, the results of *group learning* are often not the same as the results of *cooperative learning*. Consider the following scenario.

An exploration calls for groups of four students to follow directions to carry out an experiment and gather data. The group data will be combined with the rest of the class' data later.

Group 1
John and Malonie read the directions, set up the experiment, conduct the experiment, and record the data. Michael reads a science fiction book and Stacey does her history homework.

Group 2
Matt sets up the experiment without reading the directions. He looks at the photos in the book and glances at the experiment set up of the group nearest to him. Debra reads the directions to herself and notices that Matt has missed one step. She doesn't know if she should say something or not. Meanwhile, Dan looks on impassively, and Ryan wanders over to another group. Ryan helps the other group set up and complete the experiment.

These types of group interaction are common when the students and the teacher are not clear what cooperative learning is and what it isn't.

The Four Parts of Cooperative Learning

Cooperative learning is based on four basic ideas defined by Johnson and Johnson (1984). These include positive interdependence, individual accountability, cooperative skills, and assessment. Some of these ideas are clearly embedded in the *Math Thematics* curriculum, while others are achieved by teaching students appropriate social skills.

We're All In This Together!

Positive interdependence is sometimes communicated to students as "*together* you must attain this goal." Fundamentally, it means the group cannot succeed unless *all* members of the group succeed.

Sometimes positive interdependence means that students need each other to complete a task or understand a concept. Other times it means sharing materials or information.

To help students develop positive interdependence, you can assign a task or role to each group member. The list below gives some ideas for assigning tasks. Remember that not all roles are applicable for all situations.

Roles and Tasks for Group Members

- **Record-keeper** – Records the data for the group.
- **Writer** – Writes or edits the final report to be turned in.
- **Materials Dispatcher** – Gathers and distributes materials needed by the group. This student may also put away all materials at the end of the period.
- **Encourager** – Encourages everyone to participate and notes when members have done a good job. (We recommend that you assign this job to all students.)
- **Reader** – Reads the directions, story, or problem out loud.
- **Spokesperson** – Reports on the group's progress or results.
- **Time Keeper** – Monitors how much time the group has left to complete the task.
- **Noise Monitor** – Reminds group members to keep the noise level within an acceptable range.
- **Ideas Generator** – Asks questions using key words like "how," "why," and "what else" to help the group get ideas.

You Are Responsible

One criticism of cooperative learning is that one student does the work for the whole group. In reality, if cooperative learning is correctly implemented, all students are accountable for their learning and for the group results. Individual accountability can be fostered in a number of ways.

- Give points to individuals who demonstrate good social and group skills.
- Test students individually on what they have learned instead of giving a group test.
- Randomly select one group member to explain the problem and solution to the class.
- Give points to groups that demonstrate exceptional cooperation.

Getting Along

In *Joining Together*, Johnson and Johnson discuss the stages a learning group may go through to become a cohesive, effective unit. These stages include a period where group members try to determine their role in the group, followed by a period of resistance to the task or the influence of group members. In the next stages, the group begins to discover ways to work together and becomes a cohesive unit. In cooperative learning groups, students are learning how to work together, as well as learning mathematics.

Social Skills

An important aspect of cooperative learning is teaching students the social skills needed to interact in a group. One way to encourage students to think about these skills is to generate a class list of behaviors that are acceptable when working within a group. Students should include rules of conduct for listening, talking, giving help, and checking other's work.

Group size and group selection also contribute to the success of cooperative learning. Even the set up of the desks and tables can influence the outcome of group learning. Below are suggestions for each of these concerns based on our work with *Math Thematics* teachers and students.

Group Size

In the *Math Thematics* curriculum, groups either have 2, 3, or 4 students. Although groups of 5 or 6 can use cooperative learning effectively, we feel that teachers and students perform better with smaller groups. We recommend that you use groups of four, and then have students pair up with the person on their right or left for partner work. Most activities designed for three students have three obvious roles for students to play. If your class is already set up for groups of four, use one or more of the roles previously listed for the fourth person.

Group Selection

At the beginning of the school year, it may be best to have students write down one person they would like to have in their group. You can then randomly select pairs of students to create foursomes. As you get to know your students, you may want to choose the groups. Some things to consider are students' instructional level, gender ratio, ethnic background, learning disabilities, and behavioral problems. It is important to remember that some groups work well together and others do not. The personalities of the students will play a major role in how well groups work together.

Classroom Set Up

Finally, the arrangement of desks or tables should be considered when implementing cooperative learning. Students should be close enough to each other to quietly discuss the problem at hand. The noise level can be an issue if students are too far away from each other or are too close to other groups. If possible, try to have desks or tables situated so that all students can see the overhead or board easily.

How Did We Do?

At various times during a module, students should reflect on how well their group has worked together, both academically and socially. These reflections can take the form of a journal entry or a group discussion. The checklist below is another way students can assess their group's progress.

You should also give feedback to students on the social interaction you observe. Making the class aware of superior behavior helps all students model appropriate conduct. Many teachers employ a point-reward system when students work in cooperative groups. These points can be added to a test score or counted as a component of the final grade.

Other Common Concerns

How often should I use cooperative groups?

The *Math Thematics* curriculum clearly states when group work is most appropriate. In Book 1, about 35% of the explorations are structured for cooperative groups. In Book 2, about 31% of the explorations involve cooperative groups and in Book 3, about 45% involve cooperative groups. The remaining activities can be done in a variety of ways and their structure is left to the teacher. Although cooperative learning is an excellent teaching tool it should not be used to the exclusion of whole class or individual work.

Should students stay in the same groups for the entire semester?

Students should have a chance to interact with others in the class, so new groups should be formed every 4 weeks or so. Since a module in the *Math Thematics* curriculum is approximately 4 weeks long, new groups should be organized for each module.

Take It Slow

There are many facets and layers to cooperative learning, and it takes most teachers years to fully incorporate the philosophy into their classrooms. This does not mean that cooperative learning is impossible to implement, but it does take work. When introducing cooperative learning to your class, you may want to focus on one part of cooperative learning, such as positive interdependence, and later bring in the other aspects.

Think About It

Think about the behaviors of the two groups described on page 84.

- How would assigning roles have helped these groups?
- How might Ryan's actions affect his group?
- Which group do you think needs training on appropriate social skills? Why?

Cooperative Learning Evaluation Form	Always	Sometimes	Never
Everyone in our group is given a chance to talk.			
My opinions are valued by others in my group.			
I listen to others in my group without interrupting.			
Our group is able to finish the task or solve the problem in the time given.			
I understand the mathematics I learn in my group.			
Other comments:			

Adjusting for Special Needs

The *Math Thematics* curriculum was written for a broad range of academic abilities and learning styles. The goal of the program is to reach **all** students. This is accomplished through the use of cooperative groups, visual representations, manipulatives, and discovery learning. Understanding more about the different types of teaching challenges you may have in your classroom, such as students with limited English proficiency or learning disabilities, can help you adapt instruction.

In this section, we have identified areas in which teachers can adjust their teaching method or the curriculum to accommodate these special students.

Learning Styles

Students learn by seeing, hearing, and doing. Knowing that some students learn best by one of these means can help you adjust your teaching style to accommodate all learners. The learning styles associated with seeing, hearing, and doing are explained in the book *Marching to Different Drummers*.

Visual learners:
- use illustrations, diagrams, tables, and charts to help them understand and remember information.
- like to follow what a teacher is presenting with an advanced organizer that outlines the presentation.

Auditory learners:
- love class discussion. They understand by working and talking with others, and they appreciate a teacher taking time to explain something to them.
- want to talk through a problem that is difficult to understand.

Kinesthetic learners:
- want to act out a situation or make a product.
- find that when they physically do something, they understand it and they remember it.

Being aware of your students' learning styles and your teaching method can help you reach all students. Think about these questions as you prepare or teach a lesson.

- Do I write down important ideas, as well as say them aloud?
- Do my students have opportunities to act out situations, in addition to reading about them?
- Are there other ways I can present this material to appeal to different learners? video or audio tapes? speakers? field trips? plays or skits? poems or stories? art work?

Instructional Levels

Middle grade students, even those at the same grade level, are at a variety of operational levels. Some students will be at a concrete level, some at an abstract level, and some at a connecting level. At the connecting level, students begin to write symbols for the physical situation. Students at a concrete level for one concept may be at an abstract level for another concept. To accommodate for these various levels, *Math Thematics* uses hands-on, concrete models whenever possible and appropriate. We recommend that you make full use of the models, by utilizing them in later work. Pictures and symbolic representations are also shown to help students make the transition from the concrete to the symbolic.

For example, in Book 1, students are introduced to integer addition and subtraction using a bean model. Students add and subtract integers intuitively in a game, and then see pictures and symbols to represent integer addition and subtraction. Finally, students formalize the ideas with a set of "rules" for adding and subtracting integers. An example from the student pages showing part of this development is shown below.

An Example of Multiple Operational Levels

The bean models in the Example below show the relationship between the expressions 5 − (−3) and 5 + 3.

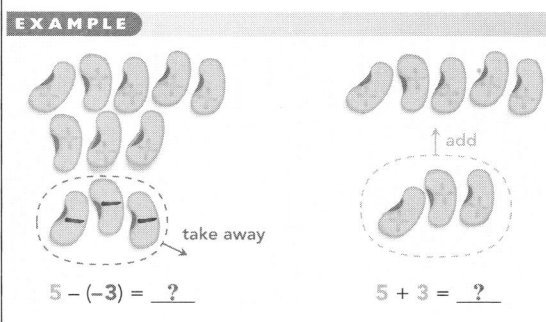

EXAMPLE

5 − (−3) = __?__   5 + 3 = __?__

22 a. In the Example above, why are 8 positive beans and 3 negative beans used to model 5?
   b. How are the expressions 5 − (−3) and 5 + 3 similar?
   c. How are the expressions different?
   d. Use the beans to find 5 − (−3) and 5 + 3. How do their values compare?

23 **Try This as a Class**
   a. Use your answers from Questions 21 and 22 to write a rule for changing a subtraction problem to an addition problem.
   b. Use your rule to find −2 − 3 by rewriting it as an addition problem.
   c. Check your answer to part (b) by using beans to find −2 − 3.

Transfer Students

Students who transfer to a school in the middle of the school year face special challenges: adjusting to a new curriculum, making friends, and adapting to new routines.

Since *Math Thematics* revisits each math topic several times during the year, there is ample time for transfer students to catch up. For example, probability is seen in four different modules in Book 2, with time in each to review the previously learned concepts. Mastery of the basic concepts of probability is not expected until the middle of the school year. In addition, the *Practice & Application Exercises* and *Spiral Review* provide opportunities to assess how much the transfer student already knows. The curriculum chart on pages 5–8 of this handbook shows how math topics are explored several times throughout the year.

The adjustment to hands-on activities with manipulatives is usually not a problem for the student. Clear expectations on the use of these materials is essential however. Transfer students may need to be instructed on the roles and responsibilities in cooperative-learning groups. These groups can help new students build friendships. For a more in-depth look at cooperative learning, see pages 84–86.

Parents new to *Math Thematics* often worry about the level and variety of mathematics. The use of cooperative learning and manipulatives may cause parents to fear that their child is doing "baby" work. It is important to inform parents about the *Math Thematics* philosophy and your own. Consider writing a letter to parents that outlines your expectations of students' work and behavior. For a sample letter on the *Math Thematics* philosophy, see page 80 of this handbook.

Language and Cultural Diversity

Students with limited English proficiency can enhance self-esteem and build friendships in cooperative-learning groups. On some occasions, the cooperative group should have two or more students who speak the same language or are from the same ethnic group. Allowing students with the same background to form a group can help the students feel accepted.

There are several ways to actively engage students in the learning process. The suggestions below apply to all students, but they are especially helpful for linguistically or culturally diverse students.

- Encourage students to discuss how the module theme relates to their lives. Many of the *Practice & Application Exercises* can be used to explore multicultural events or issues.

- The hands-on work in *Math Thematics* allows students to explore concrete models. You may want to have the manipulatives available for use at home or in later modules.

- Create a poster of troublesome mathematical words or English phrases. Try to give a translation of the word or phrase in one of the languages spoken in your class. Review these terms often and try to anticipate other difficult words students may encounter.

Be sure to involve parents through letters or conferences. Clearly state your expectations for your students and ways parents can help students succeed in school.

Learning Disabled Students

Some characteristics of a learning disabled student are hyperactivity, attention deficit, impulsiveness, and reading difficulties. Specific suggestions for these behaviors follow. The additional practice provided in the *Spiral Review* and *Extra Skill Practice* will help solidify understanding of math concepts for all students, and are extremely helpful for learning disabled students.

Hyperactive

The hands-on activities in *Math Thematics* work well with hyperactive students, but establishing well-defined goals and expectations for the activity and a student's behavior will help the hyperactive student channel his or her energy. Consider posting a class-generated list of rules and goals.

Attention Deficit

Attention deficit students are often distracted by superfluous pictures, designs, or other problems. The *Math Thematics* materials have little extraneous visuals; thus, most photos, pictures, graphs, and diagrams relate to the theme or mathematics content and are essential.

If students have trouble focusing on one problem at a time, you may want to have them create a "window," as shown below. Students with attention deficit may have less trouble concentrating with such a tool, since all other problems are blocked from view.

Any materials needed for an activity, such as labsheets, dice, pattern blocks, and so on, should be distributed when students need them. It is difficult for many middle school students to remain focused with a bag of colorful pattern blocks at hand.

Students with attention deficit may need to sit in a low-traffic area. Additionally, it may be best to seat these students away from busy bulletin boards or display centers.

Impulsiveness

Students who hastily begin activities, games, homework assignments, or tests without reading or listening to directions may need assistance. One technique is to have students read the directions and then provide the materials for an activity or game. You may want to go over the directions for tests or homework with students before distributing or assigning them.

Reading Difficulties

The reading level in *Math Thematics* is at or below grade level. The *Think About It* questions give students the opportunity to reflect on the reading. You can supplement these questions to be sure students comprehend what they have read.

A helpful organizer for students is a display of mathematical vocabulary on a wall chart or a student-created math dictionary.

Gifted Students

Math Thematics provides teachers with many projects and exercises to enrich the learning of gifted students.

Challenge exercises in the *Practice & Application Exercises* provide one source of enrichment. Often these exercises build student's problem-solving skills.

Extensions take students to a deeper level of understanding of the mathematics or they connect to other branches of mathematics.

Extended Explorations (E^2) are completed by all students but are rich activities for gifted students. Because each E^2 is open-ended, gifted students can develop creative approaches and solutions to the problem. One component of an E^2 is the presentation of the solution. Gifted students can use their expressive talents to present the solution.

Module Projects vary greatly in math content and theme. These projects can be a creative release for many gifted students, since music, artwork, and drama can be used in the projects. Creativity and divergent thinking will help students devise unusual solutions to the projects.

A Final Note

Adjusting for the special needs of students takes a team of people: the student, parents, general classroom teacher, and possibly the special education teacher, speech therapist, physical therapist, counselor, and others. The suggestions given in this section are limited and do not encompass all special needs cases. We recommend that you consult with your team to decide which of the teaching ideas are appropriate for your students.

Professional Development Handbook

Materials List for Book 1

This is a complete list of materials needed for Book 1 of *Math Thematics*. All quantities are based on a class of 30 students.

Manipulatives

A classroom set of each is needed, unless otherwise noted.

- Pattern blocks
- Geoboards with rubber bands
- Base-ten blocks
- Number cubes or dice (30)
- Chips (320 in two different colors)
- Centimeter cubes
- Plastic sticks in 2 in., 3 in., 4 in., 5 in., and 6 in. sizes. (optional)

Regular School Supplies

- Graph paper (360 sheets total, 120 sheets of centimeter graph paper)
- Unlined paper (180 sheets)
- Dot paper (30 sheets)
- Paper with non-rounded corners (30 sheets)
- Index cards (3 packages, size: 3 in. $\times$ 5 in.)
- Tracing paper (60 sheets)
- Construction paper (assorted colors)
- Poster board (8 sheets or more)
- Chalk (1 box)
- Colored pencils or markers (8 boxes)
- Scissors (15–30)
- Transparent tape
- String (about 50 ft)
- Compasses (30)

- Protractors (30)
- Rulers (15–30, customary and metric)
- Meter sticks (8)
- Yardsticks (8), only if your meter sticks do not have customary units on the back side
- Watch or clock (with a second hand)
- Glue (8 bottles)
- Paper clips (2 boxes)

Technology

- Fraction calculators (30)
- Drawing, spreadsheet, probability, and statistical software (optional)

Additional Supplies

- 1 paper bag (any size)
- Empty milk containers (sizes: $\frac{1}{2}$ pint, pint, gallon)
- Various juice bottles and cans
- Small plastic bags for storing supplies
- Pennies (375, 15 bags of 25 coins)
- Newspaper
- "Sandbag" (any object will work)
- Uncooked spaghetti (30 pieces)
- Rice (1 large bag)
- Single hole punch (8 or more)
- Paper cups (15)
- Inflatable globe
- Beans (1 bag of light-colored, uncooked beans)
- Cardboard box

- Clean trash (aluminum cans, newspaper, plastic bottles, and so on)
- Circular objects (30 or more)
- Drinking straws (96)

Science Supplies

- Graduated cylinder or measuring cup
- Scale (for measuring weight in customary units)
- Balance scale with metric weights (up to 3 kilograms)
- Eyedroppers (8)

Commonly Asked Questions

Will my students learn the "basics" in *Math Thematics*?

Yes. *Math Thematics* begins Book 1 with a review of whole number computation. Students then explore fraction, mixed number, decimal, and percent concepts. Computation, mental math, and estimation are explored and revisited throughout Book 1. Books 2 and 3 either provide review of basic number concepts in the explorations or in the *Toolbox*. These later books also extend the number concepts to negative exponents, scientific notation, square roots, percents greater than 100%, and integer computation.

Can I use *Math Thematics* modules to create interdisciplinary units? If so, which ones should I use?

Since each module of *Math Thematics* is based on a theme, many of the modules can be used as a starting place for developing an interdisciplinary unit. The modules listed below will be the easiest to implement because they already contain strong connections to science, social studies, language arts, or other subject areas. The *Teacher's Resource Book* contains complete lists of the subjects that connect to the modules.

Book 1
Module 3: Statistical Safari
Module 7: Wonders of the World
Module 8: Our Environment

Book 2
Module 2: Search and Rescue
Module 6: Flights of Fancy
Module 7: Health and Fitness

Book 3
Module 1: Amazing Feats, Facts, and Fiction
Module 3: The Mystery of Blacktail Canyon
Module 5: Inventions
Module 6: Architects and Engineers
Module 8: Making an Impact

What are some of the science topics covered in *Math Thematics*?

Math Thematics introduces many ideas from science, as shown in the chart below.

Science Topics in *Math Thematics*

Book 1

Module 1, Section 1
Identifying animal tracks

Module 2, Section 1
Spider web patterns

Module 3
(most sections have a science connection)
Fish tagging, relationship between metric units, relocating sheep, mass and length of dinosaurs

Module 6
Body ratios, jumping ability of animals

Module 8
(all sections have a science connection)
Lightning, recycling, water, meteors, air pollution

Book 2

Module 1, Section 2
Acceleration

Module 2, Section 2
Temperature and wind chill

Module 3, Section 5
Metric system

Module 5, Section 2
G-forces, elasticity

Module 6
(most sections have a science connection)
Aerodynamics, wing-loading, rigidity, relationship between metric units

Module 7
(all sections have a science connection)
Calories, heart rate, food value, exercise, sleep

Book 3

Module 1, Section 1
Space flight

Module 3
(most sections have a science connection)
Archaeology, friction, acceleration, carbon dating

Module 4, Sections 2 and 6
Phyllotaxis, deep sea searches

Module 5, Section 3
Microscopes and telescopes

Module 6
(all sections have a science connection)
Designing houses, tunnels, chairs, and theaters

Module 8, Section 1
Endangered animals

Since *Math Thematics* integrates math concepts, how will I know when mastery of a concept is expected?

Each exploration contains a *Goal* statement that tells what content will be explored. If there is a *Checkpoint* question for that goal item, then some level of mastery is expected. The *Checkpoint* will indicate what is expected. You might also look at the *Module Review and Assessment* pages. If mastery is expected, there will be one or more questions on the assessment pages with a reference to the exploration where the content was taught. If there is no *Checkpoint* question, then this content is too new or too difficult for students to have mastered. Expect to see the same content in a different application in a later module.

Why do my students have to do so much writing in *Math Thematics*?

Writing is one way for students to communicate what they understand. It is a valuable tool for you and your students. Through writing, students can solidify their mathematical knowledge. You can better assess what students know and what misconceptions they may have.

Remember that not every question requires a written answer. You may have students discuss the answer in small groups or as a class. Or you can have one group member write the answer for the group. The important part is having students communicate about and through mathematics.

How are algebra concepts developed in *Math Thematics*?

Algebra concepts are introduced on an intuitive level in Book 1. Some of the topics covered in Book 1 are coordinate graphing, integer concepts, and writing and evaluating expressions. Students also use graphs, tables, and equations to show relationships. Throughout Book 1, students work with concrete models as often as possible and whenever the models are appropriate. In Book 2, students explore algebra ideas in most of the modules. Topics include writing and solving linear equations, writing and graphing inequalities, and using formulas. Book 3 builds on the concepts explored in the earlier books. Students continue to write and solve linear equations, but they also explore quadratic and exponential equations.

I am very interested in a topic covered in Module 7 and would like to use that module earlier in the year. Will my students have the prerequisite skills to do this?

Probably not. The *Math Thematics* modules are designed to be completed in order. So moving a module forward in the year will not benefit students who do not have the prerequisite skills. This can lead to frustration for you, your students, and parents. Since much of the content is revisited several times during the year, your students will lose the gradual increase in the depth of the development. We strongly suggest that you continue through the modules as sequenced, but perhaps share your enthusiasm for a particular topic in an informal way earlier in the year.

What are the *Module Projects* and how do I use them?

The *Module Projects* are extended projects that incorporate the concepts students have learned in the module. They appear in about half of the module sections, so students will work on them 2 or 3 times throughout a module. Students complete the project at the end of the module. The final project piece is always open-ended and creativity is encouraged. Some of the projects students will work on are designing pop-up art, creating secret codes, and solving a mystery. You may choose to try one or two projects your first year teaching with *Math Thematics*. You may use them as extra credit projects, assign them to advanced students, or complete them as a class.

References

Why Change Mathematics Education?

Anderson, R., B. Anderson, et. al. *Issues of Curriculum Reform in Science, Mathematics and Higher Order Thinking Across the Disciplines.* Washington, DC: U.S. Department of Education, 1994.

Clewell, B., B. Anderson, et. al. *Breaking the Barriers.* San Francisco, CA: Jossey-Bass Publishers, 1992.

National Council of Teachers of Mathematics. *1997–98 Handbook.* Reston, VA: National Council of Teachers of Mathematics, 1997.

National Research Council. *Everybody Counts.* Washington, DC: National Research Council, 1989.

U.S. Department of Education. *Pursuing Excellence.* National Center for Education Statistics, 1996.

Presenting the Middle Grades *Math Thematics* Curriculum

National Council of Teachers of Mathematics. *Curriculum and Evaluation Standards for School Mathematics.* Reston, VA: National Council of Teachers of Mathematics, 1989.

Assessment

California State Department of Education. *A Question of Thinking.* Sacramento, CA: California State Department of Education, 1989.

Mathematical Sciences Education Board. *Measuring Up Prototypes for Mathematics Assessment.* Washington, DC: National Academy Press, 1993.

Mathematical Sciences Education Board. *Measuring What Counts.* Washington, DC: National Academy Press, 1993.

National Council of Teachers of Mathematics. *Assessment Standards for School Mathematics.* Reston, VA: National Council of Teachers of Mathematics, 1995.

National Council of Teachers of Mathematics. *Curriculum and Evaluation Standards for School Mathematics.* Reston, VA: National Council of Teachers of Mathematics, 1989.

National Council of Teachers of Mathematics. *Teaching and Learning Mathematics in the 1990s (1990 Yearbook).* Reston, VA: National Council of Teachers of Mathematics, 1990.

Stenmark, Jean Kerr, Editor. *Mathematics Assessment Myths, Models, Good Questions, and Practical Suggestions.* Reston, VA: National Council of Teachers of Mathematics, 1991.

Communicating with Parents

Cavazos, L. *Educating Our Children: Parents and Schools Together.* Washington, DC: U.S. Department of Education, 1989.

Carnegie Council on Adolescent Development. *Turning Points: Preparing American Youth for the 21st Century.* Washington, DC: Carnegie Council on Adolescent Development, 1989.

Rutherford, B., B. Anderson, et. al. *Parent and Community Involvement in Education.* Washington, DC: U.S. Department of Education, 1997.

Cooperative Learning

Bennett, B., C. Rolheiser-Bennett, and L. Stevahn, *Cooperative Learning: Where Heart Meets Mind.* Bothell, WA: Professional Development Associates, 1991.

Hill, S. and T. Hill, *The Collaborative Classroom: A Guide to Co-operative Learning.* Portsmouth, NH: Heinemann, 1990.

Johnson, D. and F. Johnson, *Joining Together: Group Theory and Group Skills.* Needham Heights, MA: Allyn and Bacon, 1991.

Johnson, D., R. Johnson, E. Holubec, et. al. *Circles of Learning: Cooperation in the Classroom.* Association for Supervision and Curriculum Development, 1984.

Johnson, D., R. Johnson, E. Holubec, et. al. *Circles of Learning: Cooperation in the Classroom.* Edina, MI: Interaction Book Company, 1990.

Slavin, R. *Cooperative Learning: Theory, Research, and Practice*. Englewood Cliffs, NJ: Prentice-Hall, Inc., 1990.

Adjusting for Special Needs

Callahan, W. (1994). "Teaching Middle School Students with Diverse Cultural Backgrounds." *The Mathematics Teacher,* 87 (February 1994): pp. 122–126.

Cuevas, G. "Increasing the Achievement and Participation of Language Minority Students in Mathematics Education." *Teaching and Learning Mathematics in the 1990s.* Reston, VA: The National Council of Teachers of Mathematics, 1990.

Cummins, J. *Empowering Culturally and Linguistically Diverse Students with Learning Problems*. Reston, VA: Council for Exceptional Children, 1991.

Guild, P. and S. Garger, *Marching to Different Drummers*. Alexandria, VA: Association for Supervision and Curriculum Development, 1985.

Hardman, M. L., C. J. Drew, and M. Winston-Egan, *Human Exceptionality: Society, School, and Family*. Needham, MA: Allyn and Bacon, 1996.

Montone, C. L. *Teaching Linguistically and Culturally Diverse Learners: Effective Programs and Practices*. Santa Cruz, CA: National Center for Research on Cultural Diversity and Second Language Learning, 1995.

National Joint Committee on Learning Disabilities. [Letter to NJCLD member organizations.] 1988.

Sovchik, R. J. *Teaching Mathematics to Children*. New York, NY: HarperCollins College Publishers, 1996.

Wood, J. W. *Adapting Instruction for the Mainstream*. Columbus, OH: Charles E. Merrill Publishing Company, 1984.

Scope & Sequence
Middle Grades Math Thematics, Book 1

The code following each item indicates the module, section, and exploration in which the topic is found. For example, the code 221 means Module 2, Section 2, Exploration 1.

NUMBER STRAND

Fractions

Topic	CODE
• Write fractions and mixed numbers to describe drawings or situations.	221
• Use a fractional part to find a whole.	222
• Recognize equivalent fractions.	231
• Find equivalent fractions.	232
• Write a fraction in lowest terms.	232
• Write numbers in tenths, hundredths, or thousandths using words, fractions, or decimals.	251
• Use equivalent fractions to write a fraction as a decimal.	322
• Understand that a fraction can be viewed as division.	342
• Write a fraction as a decimal by using a calculator to divide the numerator by the denominator.	342
• Plot fractions on a number line to show probabilities.	412
• Model and find fraction products.	431
• Use common factors to write a fraction in lowest terms.	431
• *Extension:* Divide by common factors before multiplying two fractions to find a product in lowest terms.	431
• Rewrite a fraction greater than one as a mixed number.	462
• Rewrite a mixed number as a fraction.	462
• Write a quotient as a mixed number.	462
• Compare fractions by writing equivalent fractions with a common denominator.	512
• Compare fractions by rewriting as decimals.	512
• Add and subtract fractions with the same denominator.	531
• Find common denominators to add and subtract fractions with different denominators.	531
• Find mixed number sums with regrouping.	541
• Find mixed number differences with and without regrouping, including renaming with common denominators.	542
• Use fraction form to multiply any combination of fractions, whole numbers, or mixed numbers.	552
• Find reciprocals of fractions, whole numbers, and mixed numbers.	552

Continued

Professional Development Handbook

Number strand continued   **CODE**

- Use a reciprocal to divide a whole number by a fraction. — 561
- Interpret the whole number and fractional parts of the quotient when dividing by a fraction. — 561
- Use reciprocals to divide any combination of whole numbers, fractions, or mixed numbers. — 562

Decimals

- Identify decimal place value. — 251
- Read and write decimals. — 251
- Compare and order decimals. — 252
- Add decimals. — 261
- Subtract decimals. — 262
- Round a decimal to a specific place value. — 342
- Divide a decimal by a whole number. — 351
- Append zeros to a dividend when necessary. — 351
- Divide a whole number or a decimal by a decimal. — 362
- Multiply decimals. — 441

Percent

- Understand the meaning of percent as per hundred and model percents using a 100-square grid. — 322
- Write a percent as a fraction and as a decimal. — 322
- Write a decimal in tenths or hundredths as a percent. — 322
- Use equivalent fractions to write a fraction as a percent. — 322
- Become familiar with common fraction/percent equivalents (halves, fourths, fifths, tenths). — 322
- Write a fraction as a whole percent by dividing to find a decimal and rounding the decimal form to the nearest hundredth. — 411
- Use percents to describe data. — 661
- Use a "nice" fraction and mental math to find the percent of a number. — 661
- Learn and apply the percent equivalents for thirds. — 661
- Find a percent of a number by multiplying by a decimal. — 823
- Write any percent from 1% to 100% as a decimal. — 823
- Model and write percents greater than 100%. — 832

Estimation and Mental Math

- Decide when an estimate is appropriate. — 141
- Estimate answers by rounding whole numbers. — 141

Continued

Number strand continued

	CODE
• Determine if an estimate is less than or greater than the actual answer.	141
• Use compatible numbers to find sums or products mentally.	142
• Decide when to use mental math, paper and pencil, or a calculator.	142
• Use estimation to check whether a decimal sum or difference is reasonable	262
• Multiply decimals mentally by special multipliers like 0.001 or 1000.	313
• Use mental math to find a fraction of a whole number.	321
• Use compatible numbers to estimate a decimal quotient.	351
• Use front-end estimation to estimate a whole number or decimal sum.	352
• Use trading off to find a whole number or decimal sum mentally.	352
• Recognize when a decimal product is reasonable.	441
• Estimate decimal products.	442
• Compare fractions using number sense and mental math techniques.	511
• Choose mental math, paper and pencil, or a calculator for comparing fractions.	512
• Estimate mixed number sums.	541
• Use "counting on" to mentally subtract a mixed number from a whole number.	542
• Use mental math to multiply a mixed number by a whole number.	552
• Use number sense to estimate when dividing with fractions or mixed numbers, including recognizing when the quotient will be less than or greater than 1.	562
• Use a "nice" fraction to estimate the percent or the percent of a number.	661

Ratio and Proportion

• Use ratios to compare quantities.	611
• Express a ratio three ways (using the word to, a colon, or fraction form)	611
• Recognize and write equivalent ratios.	611
• Find and use rates to make predictions.	621
• Make predictions about rates using a table.	621
• Find unit rates and use them to make predictions.	621
• Apply ratios to problems involving measurement.	631

Continued

Number strand continued

	CODE
• Write the decimal form of a ratio to make comparisons.	631
• Find and use a "nice" fraction form of a ratio to describe data and make predictions.	632
• Discover patterns in proportions.	641
• Compare cross products to determine if two ratios are equivalent.	641
• Find the missing term in a proportion.	641
• Use a proportion to solve problems and make predictions.	642
• Explore when using a proportion is or is not appropriate.	642
• Apply percents, rates, and area to explore population density.	821

Number Theory

• Discover and use the divisibility tests for 2, 3, 5, 9, and 10.	421
• List all the factors of a number.	421
• Find the greatest common factor of two or more numbers.	421
• Identify prime and composite numbers.	422
• Use a factor tree to find the prime factorization of a number.	422
• Write the prime factorization of a number using exponents.	423
• Use the greatest common factor to write a fraction in lowest terms in one step.	431
• List several multiples of a number.	461
• Find the least common multiple of two or more numbers.	461
• Use common multiples to find common denominators.	512

Algebra

• Follow the order of operations.	143
• Understand the powers of a number.	423
• Convert between standard form and exponential form.	423
• *Extension:* Use a pattern to discover the value of 2^0	423
• Use the distributive property of multiplication over addition to multiply a mixed number by a whole number.	552
• Derive and use the number π.	742
• Use integers to represent real-world situations.	761
• Show integers on a number line.	761
• Compare integers.	761
• Use a chip model to represent integers and sums of integers.	811
• Add integers.	811
• Recognize integer opposites.	811
• Use chips to model integer subtraction.	812
• Subtract integers.	812

Continued

Number strand continued | **CODE**

- *Extension:* Apply the commutative and associative properties of addition to the addition of integers. — 812
- Write numbers in scientific notation using positive exponents. — 822
- Write numbers that are in scientific notation in standard form. — 822

MEASUREMENT STRAND

Customary System

- Use benchmarks to estimate customary length. — 521
- Use a ruler to measure to the nearest inch or fraction of an inch. — 521
- Choose an appropriate customary unit or combination of units to measure a length. — 521
- Convert between customary units of length. — 522
- Add and subtract lengths measured in customary units. — 522
- Use benchmarks to estimate capacity in customary units. — 551
- Convert between customary units of capacity. — 551
- Understand how to convert between square units in the customary measurement system. — 711
- Use appropriate customary units to estimate and measure weight. — 731
- Convert between customary units of weight. — 731
- Use benchmarks to estimate Fahrenheit temperatures. — 761

Metric System

- Use benchmarks to estimate metric length and metric mass. — 312
- Use appropriate metric units to measure length and mass. — 312
- Understand the relationships among metric units. — 313
- Convert between metric units of length and between metric units of mass. — 313
- Understand how to convert between square units in the metric measurement system. — 711
- Use benchmarks to estimate Celsius temperatures. — 761
- Understand how metric units of capacity relate to cubic centimeters, cubic decimeters, and cubic meters. — 831
- Estimate capacity in metric units. — 831
- Convert between metric units of capacity. — 831

STATISTICS STRAND

Data Displays

- Interpret and make a bar graph. — 331

Continued

Statistics strand continued   **CODE**

- Interpret and make a line plot. — 332
- Choose a bar graph, line plot, or table to find information. — 332
- Interpret and make a stem-and-leaf plot. — 361
- Compare finding information from a table and from a stem-and-leaf plot. — 361
- *Extension:* Interpret a back-to-back stem-and-leaf plot. — 361
- Make a scatter plot. — 633
- Fit a line to data in a scatter plot and use it to make predictions. — 633
- Interpret and make a line graph. — 821
- Understand how changing a graph's scale can create different impressions of the data. — 851
- Choose an appropriate type of graph to use to find information or to display data. — 851
- *Extension:* Recognize when a three-dimensional graph is misleading. — 851

Data Measures

- Make predictions from a sample. — 321
- Find the range of a set of data. — 331
- Find the mean, the median, and the mode for a set of data. — 341
- Understand the differences between the mean, the median, and the mode of a set of data. — 341
- Choose the type of average most appropriate for a set of data. — 342
- Understand the effect an extreme value in the data set can have on different types of averages. — 352
- Use a stem-and-leaf plot to determine mean, median, or mode. — 361
- Decide whether an average is an appropriate way to describe a set of data and, if so, choose the best average for the situation. — 852

ALGEBRA STRAND

Expressions, Equations, and Inequalities

- Use a variable to represent an unknown value. — 452
- Write and evaluate expressions that contain variables. — 452
- Write an equation to describe a relationship, such as the relationship between the length, width, and area of a rectangle. — 452
- Write an algebraic expression for the *n*th term in a sequence of multiples. — 461
- *Extension:* Write a combined inequality — 512
- Write a related addition sentence for a subtraction problem. — 542
- Represent a rate using a verbal phrase, ratio form, and a table. — 621

Continued

Algebra strand continued

	CODE
• Use cross products to write an equation with a variable and then solve for the missing factor.	641
• Write a proportion with a variable to represent a problem situation.	642
• Write a formula with variables to describe a geometric relationship.	712
• Use the formulas for area of a parallelogram or a triangle to find a missing dimension.	713
• Solve for a missing addend or missing factor in an equation by writing a related equation using the inverse operation.	713
• Find solutions for simple inequalities with integers, such as $x < -3$.	761

Graphing and Functions

• Write a verbal rule for an input/output table and use a rule to find input and output values.	451
• Write the coordinates for points on a coordinate grid in the first quadrant.	451
• Plot ordered pairs on a coordinate grid in the first quadrant.	451
• Display input/output values on a coordinate grid to make predictions.	451
• Represent relationships in a variety of ways (drawings, tables, verbal rules, equations, and graphs).	452
• *Extension:* Graph a set of data that shows a doubling pattern.	621
• Use a table, graph, verbal rule, and equation to discover and represent the relationship between circumference and diameter.	742
• Write the coordinates for points in all four quadrants of a coordinate grid.	762
• Plot points in all four quadrants of a coordinate grid.	762

GEOMETRY STRAND

Plane Figures

• Name basic geometric figures (point, line, segment, ray).	121
• Determine when triangles can be formed using three segments.	122
• Classify triangles by the lengths of their sides.	122
• Identify acute, right, obtuse, and straight angles.	123
• Classify triangles by their angles.	123
• Know the characteristics of a polygon.	211
• Classify polygons by numbers of sides.	211
• Identify parallel line segments.	211
• Classify quadrilaterals as trapezoids, parallelograms, rhombuses, rectangles, or squares.	211
• Identify regular polygons.	212

Continued

Geometry strand continued   **CODE**

- Identify intersecting and perpendicular lines.   712
- Identify the base and height of a parallelogram.   712
- Identify the base and height of a triangle.   713
- Identify center, radius, chord, and diameter of a circle.   741
- Use a compass to draw a circle.   741
- *Extension:* Construct a hexagon using a compass and a straightedge.   741

Congruence and Similarity

- Identify figures that have line symmetry.   212
- Determine the number of lines of symmetry for a given figure.   212
- Divide a figure into congruent parts.   222
- Perform a translation, a rotation, and a reflection.   241
- Use transformations to make designs.   242
- Understand characteristics that make figures similar.   651
- Identify similar figures and their corresponding parts.   651
- Identify congruent figures.   651
- Apply similarity to solving problems involving scale drawings, scale models, and map scales. 652

Space Figures

- Recognize prisms and identify their parts.   721
- Name prisms based on the shapes of their bases.   721
- Construct space figures from nets.   722
- Develop 3D spatial visualization skills by predicting the shape a net will form.   722
- Draw a prism.   722
- Recognize pyramids.   731
- Recognize cylinders and identify their parts.   752

Measurement

- Find the area and perimeter of a rectangle.   452
- Measure and draw angles using a protractor.   653
- Use appropriate customary units to estimate and measure the area of a rectangle.   711
- Develop and apply a formula for the area of a parallelogram.   712
- Develop and apply a formula for the area of a triangle.   713
- *Extension:* Estimate the area of an irregularly shaped figure.   713
- Understand the concept of volume.   721

Continued

Geometry strand continued

	CODE
• Develop and apply a formula for the volume of a prism.	721
• Develop and apply a formula for the circumference of a circle.	742
• Estimate the area of a circle using inscribed and circumscribed squares.	751
• Develop and apply a formula for the area of a circle.	751
• Develop and apply a formula for the volume of a cylinder.	752
• *Extension:* Develop and apply a formula for the volume of a cone.	752
• Apply the formula for the volume of a rectangular prism to help visualize volumes.	823
• Apply formulas for the area of circles, rectangles, and triangles to find geometric probabilities.	841

PROBABILITY STRAND

• Find experimental probabilities and write them in fraction, decimal, and percent forms.	411
• List the set of outcomes that make up an event.	412
• Find the theoretical probability of an event.	412
• Identify impossible and certain events.	412
• Understand that probability must be between 0 and 1.	412
• Understand the concept of a fair game.	662
• Construct a tree diagram to list all the outcomes of an experiment.	662
• Use a tree diagram to determine and compare probabilities.	662
• Simulate a geometric probability situation.	841
• Find geometric probabilities.	841
• Use probability to predict.	841
• Informally explore ideas related to probabilities of complementary events.	841

DISCRETE MATHEMATICS STRAND

• Find a rule to extend a pattern.	111
• Recognize the relationship between the terms and term numbers of a sequence.	112
• Write a general rule for a sequence.	112
• Use an organized list to find the number of possible arrangements.	132
• Use logical reasoning to solve problems.	162
• Sort sets of data using a Venn diagram.	311
• Use the words *and* and *not* in describing set relationships.	311
• Apply Venn diagrams to develop ideas about common factors.	421

Continued

Discrete mathematics strand continued   **CODE**

- Follow the steps in a flowchart.   442
- Write an algebraic expression for the *n*th term in a sequence of multiples.   461

PROBLEM SOLVING STRAND

4-Step Approach

- Learn the first step in a problem solving approach—understand the problem.   131
- Identify the important information in a problem, including recognizing when too much or too little information is given.   131
- Make a plan to solve a problem.   132
- Carry out a plan to solve a problem.   133
- Complete the problem solving approach by looking back and reflecting on the problem and the solution.   133
- Extend a solution to the general case.   162
- Decide when a mixed number quotient is appropriate to solve a problem.   462

Strategies

- Make a table to organize your work.   111
- Apply problem solving strategies such as *try a simpler problem* and *make an organized list*.   132
- Choose a strategy or combination of strategies to solve a problem.   132
- Learn about team skills in problem solving.   151
- Use visual representations to help solve problems and explain solutions.   151
- Use proportions to solve problems.   642
- Use equations to solve problems.   713

Self-Assessment

- Understand and use the *Mathematical Language Scale* for self-assessment.   123
- Understand and use the *Representations Scale* for self-assessment.   151
- Understand and use the *Problem Solving Scale* for self-assessment.   161
- Understand and use the *Connections Scale* for self-assessment.   162
- Understand and use the *Presentation Scale* for self-assessment.   162